Soul Journey

Dear lovely Tamsen

Much love

Cherry 17/07/2012

x

Wilson King *Publishers*
Banbury, Oxfordshire

Soul Journey, The Greatest Secrets To Living The Life You Want
Copyright © 2012 Lisa Cherry

British Library Cataloguing in Publication Data.
A catalogue record for this book is available from the British Library.
Published in the UK by Wilson King Publishing

ISBN: 978-0956331083

Printed by Print on Demand Ltd, Peterborough
This book is printed on environmentally friendly paper

FSC PEFC

Photograph credits, Lisa Cherry
Cover design by Joy Aitman
Editor Alison Neale

All efforts have been made to observe the legal requirements with regard to the rights of suppliers of photographic and other materials.

Soul Journey

The Greatest Secrets
To Living The Life You Want

By

Lisa Cherry

"The most beautiful people we have known are those who have known defeat, known suffering, known struggle, known loss, and have found a way out of the depths.

These persons have an appreciation, sensitivity and an understanding of life that fills them with compassion, gentleness and a deep loving concern. Beautiful people do not just happen."

Elizabeth Kubler Ross

Acknowledgments

This book needed all of you and those I have not yet met. There are, of course, certain people without whom I would never have been able to get to this point. I can't mention everyone as every single human being I have met to date has contributed in some way to allow my arrival at this exact place in my life.

There are, however, people without whom this project would not have been at all possible to achieve and I thank you all from the deepest place in my heart. The unwavering support and dedication from Kirsten Hanlon, Tracey Jefferies, Gary Fox and Hannah Jago, who have become like an extended family to me, in greater and lesser degrees tackling my continuous demands and needs for clarification that I'm doing ok, will never be forgotten!

I must thank my beautiful children Zak and Saskia who haven't got a clue what I'm doing or how life changing an experience it has been. They just turn up every day to love and be loved in the hope I can give them a fiver and/or a lift. There is much to be said for this; it's very grounding!

It's imperative that I thank Alison Neale for editing my labour of love, Steve Sorbrook for patience and understanding through the design of my website, Nikki De Villiers for writing About The Author and a myriad of other pieces that I could never have written for myself and Alex Hall for neverending tolerance during the writing up of the transcripts from a Dictaphone.

I must also thank Stephen Smith who I met a matter of weeks before this project began. He has not known me in any other way than writing a book and without question he believed in me.

And finally, although most crucially, I thank all of the women who have been on this journey with me, giving of their time and this emotional space, so that this project could work. So a big thanks to Alison Neale, Ann Connor, Annett E. Bank, Amy Trevaskus, Beverley Jones, Chrissie Lewandowski, Gabby Mottershead, Jayne Hardy, Judith Haire, Julie Southgate, Kelly Short, Nikki Leader, Rachel Linstead, Rani Bilkhu, Sarah Crofts and Sue Ritchie.

*

Contents

Foreword

Lisa Cherry is an impressive woman – a mother, social worker, educator, author, therapist and an inspirational public speaker. When you get to know her life story I'm sure that, like me, you will hold her in awe.

At first sight she seems quite ordinary but you soon come to realise that here is a woman with a passion for life, a woman who is in control and a woman who is in charge of her own destiny. This has not always been the case though. When I first met Lisa, I was working (and still am) as a Caseworker for The Buttle Trust (now Buttle UK). She was a 20 year old, homeless alcoholic, trying to get her life back on track. She had recently arrived in London with just a carrier bag of possessions after leaving care a few years previously. She had reached rock bottom but somehow had realised that if she wanted to – literally - survive, she needed to change her life. She saw education as the way forward but had no money to access it. Buttle UK provided the support she needed and helped her through college and university. She has since built on that foundation and now dedicates herself to making a difference and helping women become the best they can be.

Central to everything we do at Buttle UK is the belief that all young people, however vulnerable and marginalised – just like Lisa was back then – are worth investing in through our grant aid programmes. The impact of these grants can be huge and, as evidenced by Lisa, they can help change people's lives. By supporting their education these grants give young people the power to shape their own futures and at the same time educate and inform our work. Lisa opened our eyes to the obstacles that young people leaving care face in accessing and remaining in further and higher education. Her experiences, and those of others in a similar position, helped galvanise Buttle UK into doing more to help this group and we do this today by running the Quality Mark for Further and Higher Education Institutions - a scheme which celebrates the work colleges and universities do to support young people from care.

Lisa's book is a powerful examination of the life stories of ordinary women who, like her, have overcome adversity and done amazing things. It considers the complexity of change and how through supporting and nurturing each other we can bring about change, not just in our lives, but also in the lives of others. It looks honestly at how difficult the road to recovery and wellness can be for those who have experienced such challenges and how that road should never be travelled alone.

I am extremely proud to support Lisa in her latest endeavour and congratulate her on her amazing achievements to date. I wish her even more success through her book and thank her for so generously offering to donate some of the proceeds to Buttle UK!

Karen Melton

Casework Manager, Buttle UK

Introduction

Think of this book like a photograph. It is a moment in time; nothing more and nothing less. All the stories, the interpretations of them, the way we understand them and how each of the writers has understood them, will be different now than they were in that moment that the story was captured.

The way I have understood that this book should be written today, yesterday and tomorrow will all change with every moment that has passed and with every moment that is yet to come.

I have put together this collection of stories in a certain way. The way that I have understood them and positioned them in this book is based on my knowledge, experience and understanding at the time of writing and it is that that has allowed this unique creation.

We are constantly evolving, growing, developing, experiencing and nothing, absolutely nothing, stays the same. It is with this comprehension of fluidity, movement and evolution that I would most like you to appreciate this book; without absolutes, without fixed notions of what is being said. Read this book today and then again next week. Pick it up in six months and then again after a year. Each time will show you a different message, a different story and another perspective; such is the movement of our experience, knowledge and understanding.

*

My name is Lisa Cherry and if I am to pinpoint the beginning of my recovery, my journey to wellness, the opening door to a life filled with the quest for truth and purpose and fulfilment, then it starts after yet another blackout 'drunk'. The moment of clarity that came in the deadness of my hangover on that particular day saw me flung headlong into a world of recovery, self-development and personal growth at the grand old age of twenty! I arrived at an AA meeting in the basement of a church off the Kings Road in Chelsea at 10pm on a Saturday night to be greeted by a myriad of lively characters, some full of despair and some full of hope, but all with arms open.

This first AA meeting sat comfortably and neatly on the back of a painful and difficult adolescence that had concluded through finding refuge via a very close and intimate relationship with alcohol and marijuana; they became my close friends and allies as I waded through the quicksand of my life. My teenage years had been spent in children's homes and foster homes, with a two year spell of homelessness (some of that street homeless) and as much drinking and drugging as I could muster to numb this harsh reality which, if I'm honest, all seemed like a bit of an accident!

I haven't had a drink since that first meeting back in 1990, but when I put down the drink and the drugs, I was left with me, whatever that was, and I honestly had no idea. I was about to embark upon a journey that if you'd told me I was on, for the rest of my life, I may have chosen a ditch to lie in as a much more preferable route to death at the time. A terrifyingly steep learning curve loomed before me, prompted by the painful acknowledgement that I had no real idea how to 'live', no tools and no sense of self whatsoever.

My world became focused on two or sometimes three AA meetings every day. During this time of early recovery I also went to college, and then university, as I tried to claw back my lost education. I studied with a vibrant passion, funded in part by a charity called The Buttle Trust[1] and partly through working all the remaining hours left between seminars and lectures. Two simultaneous journeys, personal and academic, electrified me and turned my world on its head, showing me endless possible new perspectives from every angle, through many different lenses.

I look back on this time in my life and realise I was such a sponge for it all. It was growth nirvana! I read every book I could for my studies and my recovery was no different. Books like "The Road Less Travelled" by M. Scott Peck and "How To Heal Your Life" by Louise Hay were read over and

---

[1] The Buttle Trust awards financial support to young people (aged 16-20) with severe social problems to help continue their further education and training. 10% of all profits from the sale of this book will be donated to their work.

The Trust supports estranged young people to complete the education or training that they are determined to achieve for a better future. By funding course costs, equipment, field trips or basic items required for day-to-day living, Buttle UK relieves the financial pressures and worries that often force these vulnerable young people to abandon their studies early.

www.buttleuk.org

over again until I understood what they were saying. (See Suggested Reading at the back of the book.) They were telling me I had to look inward; I had to look to myself for change. Nothing outside of me was going to make me well, make me better, make me live a life where I could thrive rather than survive and exist. Read that again: nothing outside of me was going to make me well. This is one of those light bulb moments that provides no other alternative than to change your very understanding of the world and how you can position yourself in your own life to move forward.

I found Louise Hay's Affirmations to be life changing as much as I believe that getting sober was the beginning of a journey of self-exploration alongside absolute honesty with myself.

Throughout the last twenty one years I have read dozens of books on self-help and recovery, constantly attempted to meditate daily, continuously attended different therapies, spoken to many people, shared many tears and stared deeply into the eyes of the emotional pain felt by myself and others. I have worked with hundreds of people who are experiencing emotional pain and distress, whilst at the same time I have grown into and learnt to live with the messy reality that is Lisa Cherry. Through all my years of working with people in distress I have seen what a person looks like when their inner flame has been all but extinguished, and I can vividly recall the face that stared back at me as I looked in the mirror all those years ago:

grey skin, eyes full of sorrow and a deep disconnection with the world.

Through reflection, learning and a continuing hunger for personal growth and self-development, I have learnt that life happens to us all. Yes, in varying degrees and yes, some people appear to suffer far more pain than anyone should reasonably have to endure, while others rest easy on more minor complaints. But I know that if we are to be truly alive, we will experience loss; we will know poor health for ourselves or others; we will see a friend before their death. We may have children, we may lose them, we will watch a life slip away before our eyes. We will have our hearts broken (quite likely more than once) and, undoubtedly, we will learn that which we need to know long after we needed to know it. This is life, a continuum of growth and learning. We can decide to consciously undertake this path to wellness and fulfilment, whether it's through self-realisation in a moment of clarity, or a trauma or event that forces us to change. Or we can simply ignore the opportunities that arise in life that will help us be the very best we can be and we can just continue using all of the distractions that society provides us with.

I chose to write this book when reflecting one day that my life experiences had been somewhat unconventional and it was a rare moment when I thought to myself, wow ... I'm amazing! And I wanted to find as many amazing women as I possibly could, women who have journeyed through the more difficult aspects of life, and throw my arms around them and say Wow! You're amazing too! And so the concept of the book was born and I travelled up and down the country meeting wonderful, inspiring women who were prepared to share their story with the sole purpose of making a difference to other people.

In this book the focus has been on women. There will be a book specifically focusing on men shortly but as we experience the world so differently, I wanted to write separate books. Writing about women is a good place for me to start. I am a woman, I focus my work on women and I have studied women. I wanted to give women a voice and in doing so, acknowledge that for much of history, the voices of women have not been recorded and validated. This is a record of women's stories and I am proud to be a part of recording them.

I have not focused my efforts on women who have become financially successful, or have created hugely successful businesses (although there are people in here to whom that has happened). It is not about the extraordinary, the women who we feel we can't connect with (although each woman in here displays her own extraordinariness). I created this book because I absolutely believe we have a duty to become the very best that we can be. I wanted to crystallise this journey in some way, the actual journey from surviving to thriving, so that you can take that journey too. It's not an elusive or abstract thing that can only be accessed by supposedly 'special' people, individuals who are strong or people of a positive disposition. It's about the amazing capabilities that we all have within us; in each and every one of us. Knowing how to find that and then knowing what to do with it is what this book is about.

It is a collection of stories from women who, regardless of their particular barriers, social structures, location, education, belief system, religion, etc., have experienced difficulties and challenges, recovered from them as best they can and then used their own experience to give something back to others, in one way or another.

Each chapter is created to take you on a journey of exploration with those who have not only survived life's challenges, but who have taken those experiences and made a positive difference to others. That is, I believe, the greatest healer of all. Some stories have been left intact and others will appear in several chapters. The chapter titles are taken from the recurring themes that the journey to wellness seems to produce. They are not exhaustive by any means but offer areas of growth that have brought the most fulfilment for the contributors and, indeed, me.

I shall leave the contributors to this book out of the introduction as each and every amazing woman has a biography at the back of the book which I hope does them the justice they so deserve. Without them, this entire project would have fallen flat on its face.

What I absolutely need for you to take away from this book is the knowledge and understanding that you really can be the best you can be. I want you to grasp the idea that all you need to have in order to have what you want for your life is the desire to have it. Let me explain. I do know and understand that when you want something badly enough, you will go and get it. I also want you to understand that you can make that decision today. You can take back ownership of your life and you can have the life that belongs to you, the life you are able to live, and the life that you are meant to live.

At the end of each chapter I have left some journeying/ journaling space for you to make notes. When I talk about using journals people often ask, "But what will I write?" This space is for you to write absolutely anything you want. You can draw pictures, write down sentences that resonated with you, thoughts that came to you that you want to remember or words that help you to articulate your feelings better. The articulation of feelings, I believe, is what will give you freedom, which is why I love using journaling as a tool for understanding our inner space and world.

Something else to consider in your reading and journaling is that the journey of growth and understanding isn't linear. We don't travel comfortably from one place to another, arriving at the next destination once - and only once - we have fully understood the lesson presented to us. No. The journey is messy and chaotic and sometimes we need to repeat what we have just learnt simply because we didn't grasp what we really needed to understand. I'm sure you've said to yourself 'How did I end up here, again?!' even when you thought you'd done everything in your power to prevent a repeat situation. We also learn at different times, in different ways and hear different things, so we might understand something in different ways each time we look at it or read about it. We may think that we have grasped something but it is only one angle of it. It's complex and layered and variable.

But it is through this process that we recover and grow and learn - and we can end up with wisdom about ourselves and ultimately about others which will then lead us to an understanding that essentially the core part of the human condition is kind, non-judgemental and filled with love.

It is through this process that we learn not to judge ourselves so harshly and therefore judge others less too, remembering all the time that we can only know what we know when we know it. My exploration in this book is that of what truly fascinates me, which is how we live our journey.

And finally, please understand that all of the areas and chapters that I explore are done so in an outline fashion. I have only touched upon each 'theme', as each of the areas that I explore have so much writing, research, exploration and literature about them. I would therefore urge you to read further about anything that resonates with you or compels you to think more deeply. In this regard, I can only offer an introduction, coupled with an insight of my own experiences and those of the contributors of how their lives have been impacted upon through working through the areas of recovery, healing and personal growth.

*

Chapter One – We Came To Understand

You can probably pinpoint that moment in time when you arrived at a place of despair and experienced a longing for something to change. For some, this happens in a moment while for others it is a long and arduous road. But that moment of consciousness is a precious gift that opens doors that only operate one way. Once you walk through the door from unconsciousness to consciousness you enter a place of self-awareness and there is no way back. Just as we cannot know what we know until we know it, what we know cannot become unknown once we know it! To perform the latter is known as denial; this is the active seeking of ignorance towards a known piece of information. For example, the alcoholic may know they have a problem with alcohol but can convince themselves that "It's not that bad really, everyone does it". The over eater can use the power of denial to omit all of the food eaten while cooking or in between meals. Denial is powerful, but it is not to be confused with 'not knowing'.

I worked for many years in Social Services and Education with hurt, bewildered and disaffected young people and their families. In more recent years, I have been running a busy practice working with women as a Health and Well-being Therapist. Throughout my work, I have heard and seen recurring themes of dissatisfaction, apathy with life, or sometimes an inner deadness which, if I were to visualise it, would look like a candle losing its fight to stay lit in the wind. There is a dis-connect with life itself, the gift of life and how we as human beings engage and connect with it.

The manifestation of this shows itself in many ways and making change can feel so daunting sometimes. It's easy for people to feel trapped and unable to create change. It's all very well saying 'Make today the day for change' – which, incidentally, I say rather a lot – but sometimes there is a need for something to shift before change can even begin to take place.

We can break down the sense of disconnect we might experience with life and our feeling of lack of purpose and fulfilment; we could say that we have the feelings, the behaviour and the life consequences. So we have the way it feels to be 'me' which might be feeling trapped, alone, needy, co-dependent, apathetic, numb, joyless and disconnected. Then there is the resulting behaviour whereby we seek to rectify or remedy our feelings, or even numb them. We have many options for this in our society – drink, drugs, sex, soap operas, over eating, anything really that can be done to excess and can be used to temporarily eradicate the feelings described above.

In our day to day lives the external manifestation of our feelings and behaviour is the consequence. The consequence of all of that might look like a poorly functioning relationship that doesn't work any more - but staying is easier than leaving. Or maybe you're in a job that brings no satisfaction other than it pays the bills. Your rut, your routine, is so fixed that you have no awareness of what you are doing; you're on auto pilot, you're not fully conscious but you know on some level that this can't be right as all of this is underpinned by poor food choices, drinking too much, etc etc. There's a sense of limitation, a lack of creativity and a constriction imposed by unwritten rules that have crept into the subconscious and become a permanent rhetoric which has taken over all aspects of your being. These 'rules' keep you in your job, within your relationship, staring at the lives on TV rather than living your own life. The feelings, the behaviour used to manage them and the consequences of it all, become a mess. The knowledge of where it all starts and ends is not present....life has just become what life has become, with a circular, spiralling sense of destruction which is the sentiment behind the expressions, feeling like I'm on a hamster wheel, the rat race, a treadmill.

This sense of powerlessness shows itself in a number of the stories you are about to read, and the subsequent changes that took place once the emotional, physical and spiritual wall were in place with no way around them. I have come to see that there is often a pattern to a destructive way of life.

Through my own recovery, through the stories of the book's contributors and throughout my work, I have also come to see a pattern of the journey to wellness with recurring themes of recovery. For many of us, something happens. Something happens in our lives that means we cannot continue, we simply cannot go on the way we are. For me, it was my drinking and the mess of 'me' that I was left with when the anaesthetic had been removed. For others it may be an illness, a divorce or a bereavement, or simply a dawning that this can't be it, this can't be all there is to life! For some, the process is slow and continuing and not necessarily triggered by a major life event. The stories that unfold throughout this book tell of many paths to living consciously and purposefully, with a passion for living that knows no bounds.

Since that first seed of consciousness was sown 21 years ago I have had many moments as powerful as that first burst of awareness, and each moment has opened up a new stage of my journey and a new part of myself. Each time I have been thrown into the den of greater self-awareness. The really meaningful growing and learning hasn't come from the work I have done while pottering about in the self-help section of most bookshops, but from gut wrenching, knee wobbling, emotional tormented agony. In other words, I've done the hardest work when I've had to. "You must do the thing you think you cannot do." Eleanor Roosevelt.

I didn't wake up one day and think to myself, let the pain begin. Let today be the day when I face up to all my demons, confront all that it is to be 'me', sob like a small child wanting something they can't have for weeks on end and endure a continuous sensation of suffocation in the solar plexus area of my chest (oh have I felt emotional pain!) "Truth or reality is avoided when it is painful.....we must be totally dedicated to the truth. Conversely, we must always consider our personal discomfort relatively unimportant and, indeed, even welcome it in the service of the search for truth." Dr Scott Peck.

This knowledge seemed incomprehensible to me once, but I now welcome this movement through learning and growth and understand it to be The Healing Response (sometimes known as the Healing Crisis). This is a 'state' used in holistic therapies to describe the way the body responds to treatments. Whatever is trapped in the body will be released through the therapy. So for example, physically this might manifest through headaches, going to the toilet more or feeling tired. Emotionally, this may appear via crying, feeling 'down' or feeling euphoric even. I believe that working through your emotional pain is no different. It's about change and growth and the body, mind and spirit need to adjust accordingly to all of the new information; it's almost like undergoing a re-wiring of you, learning and unlearning years of information and untruths.

I always welcome the healing response as I know that what follows is a deepening in my development, happiness and reliance on my inner self for acceptance, love and belonging. It's not always comfortable but once you understand that it's part of the process, it can be seen as a positive thing.

When change is occurring within us, when growth is the only outcome of the pain, this is part of the healing response. Things often appear to get worse before they get better. In holistic therapies we talk about this a lot as it is the body's way of eliminating toxins on a physical level, but emotionally it is a form of release of all the negative feelings we trap in the body. I have found this to be true of working through emotional pain in any capacity. It hurts, I hurt, I understand something, something within me shifts and I feel better. But it is because of this process of 'feeling' that people often go into denial or slump further into negative behaviour patterns, keeping them stuck and increasing their sense of disconnectedness. This is what Dr Peck so aptly points out in the quote above because essentially, it is a natural thing to want to avoid pain. But when you have been through the process a few times, you will come to a place of trust and understanding as you recognise that it is part of the way forward. Inevitably, what happens is that avoidance becomes more painful than change, rendering it preferable to deal with all that needs dealing with.

For whatever reason you picked up this book, wherever you are on your journey, the most important thread that connects us in this process is the understanding that we all have choices and we can therefore all make changes. As our arrival at this point will be different, so will our recovery process or journey into consciousness be. Our perspectives are all different too. One person's crisis is another person's opportunity for change. What can be too much to deal with for one person can be fairly insignificant to another and that difference between us all must absolutely be respected.

We are never without choices although I can see that look of hostility and despair when I say that to someone who feels with utter conviction that there is absolutely no choice for them as they are settled so deeply in their pain. The frustration within myself when I have rendered myself 'choiceless' is unbearable and of course it is indeed a nonsense. There are always choices, it's just that some of them are not great; in fact, some of them are just not nice at all, but they are a choice nonetheless. Making a choice and then living with the consequences of that, taking responsibility, is what it is to be a grown up. And sometimes it would be nice to have a day off from that, wouldn't it? But that is not the option on this path of learning, growing, developing and seeking the truth. There are no days off but the rewards have never ceased to amaze me.

Personal responsibility does appear to cause some people great difficulty. I cannot state clearly enough the importance of this in our own role to creating personal change. No one can do it for you; it is for you to do. "Even if you're on the right path, you'll get run over if you just sit there." – Will Rogers. In other words, all the reading, thinking, wishing and hoping will not create what you need if it is not accompanied by action. If you've been struggling with change, action or choices, my greatest desire is that this book will inspire and motivate you, that it will ignite something within you and that the people you will read about will facilitate a thirst in you to move forward on your path, wherever that may lead. So I say again, no one can do it for you; it is for you to do and there is no person, no place and no thing to which you can hand over the responsibility for not doing it. When you truly grasp this, you take hold of your own power and you are therefore no longer rendered powerless.

The pain that has been felt by the women who have contributed through their life experiences is not what has intrigued me in my writing; rather it's the recurring themes within their recovery that they have tended to share. The unique collection of real life stories that awaits you in this book will inspire you. Women like you, and women like me, and women like lots of women you and I know, share their journey through life's challenges and reveal how, through working through some common themes, they found change, growth, fulfilment and a sense of purpose. These 'secrets' are now recorded in the written word for all to see, shared by a few to be read by many.

*

Personal Ramblings

Chapter Two – Creating the Fabric

I want to be clear that no one, no book, no friend can tell you when you have reached the end of the line. When you are truly sick and tired of being sick and tired, only you will know that you have arrived in this space. You will feel it within the very core of yourself. It will stare back at you each time you look in the mirror. You may well be ravaged by depression, addiction or unable to function in your daily life. You will know whether you have been here before, or whether you are nearing this point or are staring into the eyes of life and seeing nothing but a void.

I will always remain desperately grateful that I had to deal with so much pain before the age of 20. This has meant that my children have never had to see me drunk, hungover or in any one of the dangerous places that alcohol took me to.

The other major benefit of being so young when I first walked into an AA meeting and started upon my path of recovery was that I was young and hungry for this new way of life and it started me on the path that I shall walk, run and saunter along for the rest of my life. There is no going back. I have had to deal with life and all that it throws at us in its rawest form since then, but that first step into a life of consciousness and growth will always remain an anchor and a defining moment in my life, for the rest of my life.

I have read many books to help me make sense of my inner world, my relationships, my purpose and my passion. There is an extensive range from which to choose and I remember spending an inordinate amount of Saturday afternoons sitting cross-legged in the self-help section of the book shop searching for the answers, all the answers. In writing this book one of the first things I did was get onto Amazon and buy lots of books in the same genre, used ones for very little money. Few of them impressed me.

I found that there are lots of books that are authoritative or academic; they are hard work to read, provide lots of data and research, a scientifically based formula and a sense of 'them and us'. The writer talks in the third person and shares little of their own experience, thus detaching themselves from the very existence of 'living', which opens up all sorts of questions for me about their ability to understand their own journey. My preference is to read about real life, real people and real recovery. We are all unique and individual so while there are general themes of a journey to wellness, each of those themes will be interpreted differently by each and every one of us.

Some of the books are political, which I didn't want this to be. I could quite easily have gone down that road as some of the particular life experiences which come up cannot be separated from those that are unique to women living in the society in which we live. That exploration may be for another book, but it is not for this one.

There were a plethora of books that are clearly out to make money - fast! "Ten Facts That Will Change Your Life In 3 Weeks" and "Read This Book – Make Millions and Be

The Most Popular Person on The Planet". Ok I'm being facetious - but you take my point.

When I started on this process, I wanted to create something different, something that highlighted the many paths we can all take, seen through the vehicle of storytelling, which is something women love to do. We are, after all, natural storytellers and listeners. I wanted to create something collaborative and generous and honest that allows for the expression and articulation of emotion in a real and positive and accessible way. As it turns out, of course, there are lots of books out there that do this but my book, like each cake you make or conversation you have or smile you give, is unique and captures this particular moment in time.

The stories in this book, which will interweave through each chapter, are the experiences, knowledge and honest accounts of how women have brought about personal change. These are women that you will recognise, women like you or someone you know or someone you want to know. And while I have consistently called all the women involved in the making of this book "amazing", I urge you to find your own amazingness. It comes in many shapes and sizes and has no formula. If you have picked up this book, you are already in a place of "amazing" because I believe that you want change and you want connection and you want validation: validation that you are applying all the tools, skills and knowledge that you can in order that you shall thrive so that you can be the very best that you can be for the short time that you have here in this life. Your own amazingness can be found through the very process of recognising the achievements of someone else.

How did I choose the title?

When I first decided I would write a book, the title seemed to compel me to endless hours of saying a multitude of words out loud, playing with words and finding a flow that made sense. If you've had a baby, you'll understand this process and it really is not dissimilar. The title started out as Mantras of the Thriving. It made sense to me on so many levels and fitted nicely with the message I wanted to convey. The words 'Mantra' and 'Thriving' stood out to me as a cohesive way of understanding our journeys because they signified an action and an outcome and that felt positive, meaningful and achievable.

mantra [man-truh] *n.* 1. *an often repeated word, phrase, truism* 2. *that which creates a spiritual transformation within*

So a mantra is a powerful affirmation, a lesson or driving force that not only taps into your positive thinking but helps you create the life you *truly* want. It is within your grasp because it is you who creates and speaks your mantra. Because it is for you to do this, this is in essence what personal responsibility is. As I've already said, no one can do this for you.

thriving *v. To prosper, flourish, succeed, grow stronger, boom. To become very successful, happy, or healthy. To thrive means to grow strong and healthy.*

During the course of my research and in the initial stages of discussing who I would like to contribute to this book I spoke to someone who referred to themselves as a survivor. My reaction to this was one of feeling physically and emotionally uncomfortable, especially as they were talking about something that had happened over 30 years ago! For me, the term "survivor" is very useful post-trauma but has no place as a 'label' to be held onto for years after an event. It conjures up an image of a life half lived, a life not fully achieved; a life lived in pain, in a permanent state of 'getting over it', a life defined by an experience and nothing more. It is not a way of life I would aspire to, and I wouldn't like to define myself by something that happened many years ago. Caroline Myss describes this state of endlessly surviving as "woundology". As she puts it, "We are not meant to stay wounded. We are supposed to move through our tragedies and challenges and to help each other move through the many painful episodes in our lives." [2]

However, thriving is, for me, as far away from surviving as you can get. If you thrive you are being the very best you can be, finding out who you really are so you can achieve your dreams and aspirations. When you thrive you have a high regard for yourself and high self-esteem, and you're able to give back to others from the experiences that you have had, to enable others to grow and be the best they can be.

---

[2] Taken from Why People Don't Heal and How They Can by Caroline Myss

So the title I initially chose reflected the very ethos of all that underpins the book. However, I started to feel uncomfortable about the title as I asked people their reactions to it and they seemed unsure about the word mantra; there was confusion about what it meant. So with lots of help from my friends, I worked my way down to three titles and then asked people again to choose what made sense to them, what made them want to know more. I had to let go of my title and create something that had more meaning to others. Rather than hold on to my 'baby', my creation, I put it back firmly where it belongs, with you; you the reader, you the contributor, you the woman. Soul Journey – The Greatest Secrets to The Life You Want was born.

How did I choose the contributors?

The women taking part in this project were either chosen or approached directly by me or they contacted me in response to my requests for contributors on my website and social networking sites. Some people were filtered out early on as we felt our energies weren't right or they felt they needed anonymity, which was not what I wanted at all for this project. However, I absolutely respect that need to protect stories, particularly where there are children involved who may end up reading about things that affect their view of their own childhood or family members. For example, the written word is not the right place to find out for the first time about your mother's abuse. Through initial discussions, it was easily established whether or not people had really moved on from their traumas. While being involved in the project has absolutely been a journey for everyone, this was not the place to work through unresolved issues. Knowing that the process may bring up unexpected emotions, I asked everyone to ensure that their personal and professional support networks were in place, should they be required. Sensitivity, respect and clear communication has been part of the relationship between the contributors and me from the moment we connected and this has been crucial. Trust has been everything from their perspective of course, but also from mine.

Throughout the process I trusted that the right women would be sent to me, bringing their own unique qualities, experiences and energy and this is exactly what happened. What I hoped I would find - and what I did find - was that there were recurring themes and repeated actions, beliefs, mantras and patterns of behaviour. I decided to order the chapters along a 'timeline' of recovery - or of living - in order to give you, the reader, different ways of understanding. For example, one person's explanation of forgiveness may not resonate with you at all and yet another's may well give you the understanding that you have craved for a long time. I wanted to give the reader as many opportunities as possible to understand each area of healing or recovery.

Each woman does not appear in every single chapter but rather I have used elements and parts of their unique stories and weaved them through the chapters. Some of the stories felt like they had an obvious place and I have kept those in 'one piece', as to break them into sections didn't feel right and their key messages to the reader would have been lost.

To make this happen, I knew I wanted to bring together some of the most amazing women that I could in order to connect us all together and enable the understanding that we are all the same. We all have the capacity to change and grow and no one woman is stronger, more able or better than anyone else in that regard. We may all have different stories, face different challenges, have different choices (some harder than others) and different support networks, but change is available to us all, when we accept that and take it. Because when all is said and done, what we actually seek in order for our lives to be fulfilling, valuable and creative comes from within, not from without. Understand that, and the world becomes a very different place.

The women who contributed to this book have personal experiences that span destitution, recovery from cancer, living with dyslexia, domestic and sexual violence, mental illness, alcoholism, debilitating health, neglect and divorce.

"Show me someone who has done something worthwhile and I'll show you someone who has overcome adversity." - Lou Holtz

One of the areas that I really wanted to explore was around making a difference. For me, it's not only about recovering and thriving from our experiences, but also about what we do with them. How do we use those experiences to give something back to others, to make a difference, to be part of creating change? Again, I have chosen a variety of ways in which this has been achieved, from setting up a national charity to setting up support groups, and much more in between.

I deliberately wanted to include a variety of stories, recoveries and experiences because it is these stories and experiences that make us who we are and we all experience life differently and understand things differently. My research of the women included in this book verifies my belief that there are similarities in how we can live the best life that we can and that the ways in which we do this are similar. However, because we are all different, the ways in which we *understand* are different. People, places and things all come into our lives to teach us but we see and learn and grow only when we are ready. By providing a variety of stories, my thinking was that maybe, just maybe, seeing things from many perspectives would help the process of personal discovery, self-awareness, development and healing.

Make no mistake, undertaking to gain consciousness through peeling back the layers of belief systems, firmly guarded assumptions and perceptions of reality one at a time takes courage and determination. However straightforward or easy the written word allows some of these journeys to appear every single person in this book will have recollections of loneliness and frustration on their journey to the point they find themselves at today. The journey of which I speak is not available in "three easy steps" or by following "ten top tips." But it is yours for the taking; all you have to do is to want it.

Pain is inevitable, suffering is self-inflicted[3] and to actively resist change is indeed a self-imposed sufferance. "Many people confuse pain with suffering. We have to realize, first of all, that pain is not the same as suffering. Left to itself, the body discharges pain spontaneously, letting go of it the moment that the underlying cause is healed. Suffering is pain that we hold on to. It comes from the mind's mysterious instinct to believe that pain is good, or that it cannot be escaped, or that the person deserves it. If none of these were present, suffering would not exist. It takes force of mind to create suffering, a blend of belief and perception that the one thinks one has no control over. But as inescapable as suffering may appear to be, what brings escape is not attacking the suffering itself but getting at the unreality that makes us cling to pain." Deepak Chopra.

This is not to say that pain is the only path to change, or that endless hours on the couch going over and over the pain is the only place to start. Equally, as mentioned earlier, I don't personally believe there are quick fixes. There is a desire for change, there are actions to be taken, learning to be had and messages to be carried over to those around us. This is a process that takes as long as it takes for each person. The messages you'll hear from the women in this book come from a place that does not seek

---

[3] Deepak Chopra – Questions and answers website, originating from Buddhist teachings.

to judge, punish, criticise or claim to be the pedagogy. There is an entire chapter on self-love and part of that is allowing yourself the space to heal, grow and develop in a way that is nurturing and safe, surrounded by acknowledging the acceptance that it will take as long as it takes.

*

Personal Ramblings

Chapter Three – Taking the Leap of Faith

"When I let go of what I am, I become what I might be."

Lao Tzu

Are you ready to begin?

Where is the beginning? If this book were to offer you a timeline of recovery or an order of events that would lead you to a place, a destination, an arrival point, where would it start?

I ask this as we refer to life as a 'journey' and I talk about the 'journey to wellness' in this book. When I talk about 'wellness', I am referring to the whole part of you: your mind, body and spirit and your emotional wellness; your resilience in managing 'life' and its contents. The journey through life doesn't have a defined starting place and destination. There are stops and starts and places of interest and places that distract us or hold us a while to teach us something. If I'm honest, I desperately wanted to start each chapter as though it was all a process where each aspect of learning and recovery followed neatly on from the other. In doing this I could make it look compact, tidy and straightforward, thereby rendering it easy and instantly accessible; like buying a ticket to go on holiday. But in acknowledging and understanding that this is not an orderly process, a timeline, a series of places we visit one after the other, we can then start to understand the process as more chaotic and individual than some of the other books I've read would have us believe.

So for the purposes of this book, the beginning can merely be the point at which we say, I can't do this anymore. It can be the point at which the pain of not doing anything supersedes the pain of taking action. It is the point at which we choose creating change and walking down a completely different path over continuing to live a life half lived. Dr Scott Peck didn't name his bestseller The Road Less Travelled without good reason. It's a road that will be avoided by most, taken by some and unknown to others. The question is really whether or not you want to take those steps and walk down that higgledy piggledy road of cobblestones, gates and mazes. My belief is that we are dragged there kicking and screaming because the pain is so great – though the sensible ones among us will take the decision to do this without the screaming! Now I walk the path calmly and in peace, but initially it wasn't like that at all. I was dragged!

The main purpose of this book, the vision that I had for it when I first conceived of it, was to help clarify in some way how you can have the life you deserve to have. I feel that in my own journey, what I really want to do is help you to have what I have found: a way of living that is filled with gratitude, joy and a desire to live each moment with an appreciation that some people may never experience unless they were told they only had a day left to live.

It is not through reading a hundred books while gazing at your belly button or spending endless money on continuing the process of not accepting yourself (think plastic surgery) that you will find this; nor by how much money you have in the bank or who you might be married to or what type of house you live in or car you drive. There is only one place that peace, happiness and acceptance come from - and that is from within. When we have sorted all of that out, the doors are open to abundance of a different kind and suddenly the people around you and the opportunities that come your way will all reflect what is within yourself: a deep sense of self-appreciation, self-love and gratitude which allow you to have fulfilling relationships, work that is borne out of your passion, a sense of purpose and a better understanding of what it is to be human and live with compassion for yourself and others.

It's easiest to think of this in terms of a mirror that reflects back to us what is inside us. The theory goes that if you have a lot of negativity within you, you will probably be more likely to be surrounded by negativity. If you believe that you only deserve to have a job that pays your bills as opposed to one that fulfils you, then that is likely what will happen. It's like the self-fulfilling prophecy defined originally by Robert Merton: "a false definition of a situation evoking a new behaviour which makes the original false conception come true." [4] Understanding this is key as it helps us understand how much we create for ourselves (or don't) which then gives us the responsibility

---

[4] The term "self-fulfilling prophecy" (SFP) was coined in 1948 by Robert Merton in a sociological sense which looks at structures in society. I'm looking at it from an individual perspective of how this thinking impacts directly upon your life.

and the 'power' to do something about it and create change - change of such profound proportions that you will never be the same again, nor would you wish to be.

"Have a bias towards action...break that big plan into small steps and take that first step right away." -Indira Gandhi

In writing this chapter, I put together a manifesto, The Soul Journey Manifesto, a vision and a commitment to what I want to bring to you out of and within this book and also for you to take for yourself and implement into your life. Because without a vision and a commitment, you haven't got change - you have a wish. Change needs clarity and direction and passion to thrive in.

THE SOUL JOURNEY MANIFESTO

- To find passion and purpose by trying out lots of things we've always wanted to do so we can see what makes our eyes light up
- To concentrate on the thoughts and actions of overcoming adversity rather than just on the achievement itself
- To bring together women to share their stories to help and inspire others
- To provide a platform from which women can begin the process of helping themselves
- To help women believe that they can be the very best they can be - helping them to get past the greyness of what life has thrown at them
- To strive towards being in thriving mode rather than surviving mode

- To provide the evidence that everyone is amazing and strong and courageous
- To make 'self-help' about celebration of our journeys, not about rock bottom, failure or disempowerment
- To grasp that it is in our vulnerability that we will find our true strength
- To understand the value of experience and take responsibility to learn from those events, share what we have learnt and do what we can to ensure that other women have access to learn from our experiences in a meaningful and accessible way
- To have the strength to know that when an opportunity presents itself to us, we value ourselves enough to grab it!
- To deliver to you the 'ordinary' women of this world who are doing amazing things in their everyday lives
- To understand that there are amazing women everywhere all over the world living with unimaginable adversity and hardship who may never have a voice and that in acknowledging this we connect with one another, develop a strong sense of gratitude and seek to try and make a difference whenever we can

All of the above came about through asking the contributors why they chose to be involved in this project and also from my own goals and vision for pulling together this book. What I also wanted to convey and help people recognise is that within recovery, as I have said previously, there are recurring themes, all of which I will explore throughout the book. Through the interviews with the contributors, my own experience of recovery and in my work and general observations of those around me, it has become very clear that there are certain aspects of growth and personal change that are a part of each story that I hear. A positive outlook, giving for giving's sake, taking some sort of spiritual path and learning the art of self-love through having a relationship with yourself, alongside a big dollop of determination, is a good place to start. There are things that appear to be universal tenets of getting 'well'. This is very good news indeed.

It was this suspected pattern that was one of the main reasons for wanting to write this book as I believed that there are a series of beliefs, a method of change. However, telling that narrative from the position of some sort of 'person in the know' or 'expert' held no appeal to me, largely because I don't view myself in that way. It felt far more compelling to explore the issues through the stories and lives of others who have been through adversity and recovered and gone on to lead fulfilling, abundant lives full of a passion to make a difference. As I suspected, I learned that yes, no matter who we are, there are things that we have all done, all been through and all worked hard to learn and relearn and that demonstrates a formula of sorts, a pattern. The good news is this book shares that formula with you so that you too can fully enjoy and appreciate the gift that is life.

This I do know: to create change, we must do it for ourselves and we can only do it for ourselves. In other words, no other person can do this for you. I will repeat this often as understanding this is the catalyst to profound change.

Using the Chapters

The following chapters are based on what the contributors and I have learnt and observed about living the best life you can. They are not in any particular order, because I have concluded that there isn't really an order; not to our lives, our recovery or any aspect of our journey.

I have tried to start at some sort of beginning of a journey towards change, but thereafter the chapters can be used in the order they are needed. This means that you can open the book wherever you wish, should you choose to do so.

For example, different things happen at different points in our lives that can bring issues to the fore, sometimes issues that we had previously thought we'd dealt with. The big life changers death, debt and divorce can bring on a whole heap of unresolved tensions and hurts. Having children can be an incredibly large mirror reflecting back to us our own traumas and experiences of being a child and being parented. Even when I had worked through lots of areas of distress, there was something very poignant for me in looking into the eyes of my first baby and wondering what my own mother's experience had been when looking into my eyes as a baby and at that point I felt with certainty that our experiences of mothering would bear no relation to each other.

"One's real life is often the life that one does not lead."

Oscar Wilde

This is your time. It's time to take the road ahead and create the change that is possible to enable you to live a conscious life, grounded in a sense of fulfilment that can only be achieved when you are truly living the life you are meant to have - your real life, not the life of another or a ghost of yourself!

*

Personal Ramblings

Chapter Four – How did I get here?

"In order to change, we must be sick and tired of being sick and tired."

In a way this is the beginning, even though it's likely that the beginning may have started long before the actual point of surrender or change or acknowledgement that we can't take it anymore. There is that point in time when we absolutely know we can't go on.

There have been a number of times in my life where I have been in emotional pain in that place where I absolutely have to change, grow, learn, develop but my first fall to the ground was unmistakably and completely life changing.

Change can come through experiences that take us to our knees, forcing us through something to say enough is enough, I cannot go on like this because this is not ok. However, there are other times where, seemingly out of nowhere, our whole world is turned on its head.

It was December 1990 and I came into consciousness around 3am, yet again in a confused state as to where I was, who I was with and how I got there. Blackout drinking is vile. I have since met people in AA meetings who have killed another in a blackout and have no recollection of what they were doing. Imagine standing in a courtroom charged with murder and yet not knowing anything about the what, the why and the how of the situation? I woke up again at 5am, still drunk and confused and unclear as to what had happened the night before, to get ready for some desperately awful agency work which was putting food on the table at the time.

I absolutely knew, in that moment, that I couldn't go on. The sensation of nothingness within me was all-consuming and I was scared. Scared that I would die very soon if I didn't do something. When I arrived home that afternoon, still physically shaking, I picked up the Yellow Pages and called Alcoholics Anonymous. I had never heard of AA, knew nothing about it or anyone who had been. Yet something inside me knew what to do. Call it divine intervention or the universe, my gratitude knows no bounds. That evening, in a basement room just off the Kings Road in Chelsea, I sat in an AA meeting and I haven't had a drink since.

If you have picked up this book, it is likely that you have been in this place of despair and no return. Or maybe you're in it now and you want to make sure. My moment of clarity came at the end of a long line of intense pain and distress from my adolescence. For some people, this might happen less dramatically. It might happen later in life. It might arrive on the back of lots of 'stuffed down' pain and feel like it comes from nowhere or it might a momentary insight, a gift from the Universe.

*

I had been using my blog, Twitter and Facebook to tell people about this book and what I was doing and I got a phone call from Gabby who said she thought her story might be of interest to me. She had a lovely voice and sounded very down to earth as she shared her story and the catalyst which changed the direction of her life completely.

"I had a difficult childhood and by the time I was 15 years old I was pregnant and in an abusive relationship. I was placed in the care of the local authority. I was sent off to a mother and baby home in Colchester to have the baby, and it was the happiest time of my life. I loved helping the other girls with their babies and I quickly learnt how to make feeds and fold terry nappies. When my son Justin was born I fell completely in love with him and was determined to make a good life for us both. After he was born I was given a flat, but the violence returned into our lives and I fled. I left with my baby, a suitcase and a pram, returning to Manchester where I had two relatives - my grandmother, who was a paranoid schizophrenic, and an aunt who had other issues. When I was 18 I met Paul, my husband. We have been together now for 30 years, and he has given me love and stability, as well as a large extended family who I love dearly.

I started work in an office as we had ambitions to own our own house. I found I was very good at finance and administration and I worked hard, studied at night school and got several promotions. I had another baby, Liam, and returned to work when he was just nine weeks old, something I now regret. At the age of 39 I got a role as a director of a large company and I graduated with my MBA. To an outsider I guess I looked very successful; I had a great salary and a very flash company car. Internally though I was still a seething mass of insecurities. I was in awe of people I worked with and was terrified that they would discover that I wasn't as good as them; I have heard this referred to as 'imposter syndrome', and believe a lot of women struggle with this lack of self-belief. I continued to work hard, and despite being made redundant three times I kept moving from job to job, looking for my work to fulfil my need for recognition and status.

Aged 44, I was in a temporary job when I was diagnosed with Inflammatory Breast Cancer, the most aggressive and fatal type of breast cancer. IBC is known as the silent killer. It does not present with a lump; my symptoms were a thickening of the skin on my breast, and I was lucky enough to be diagnosed immediately after hospital tests. I have since met other IBC patients who were misdiagnosed for too long, by which time the cancer had spread. I was plunged immediately into the very scary world of high dose chemotherapy, mastectomy, radiotherapy and reconstruction. I started to look for the reason that this had happened to me and I knew it was the stress of my working life.

I read this quote and realised it applied to me: *It's incredibly easy to get caught up in an activity trap, in the busy-ness of life, to work harder and harder at climbing the ladder of success only to discover it's leaning against the wrong wall.* Steven Covey

I embarked upon a journey of holistic therapies to support my medical treatment and saw a healer who introduced me to Theta Healing and the Healing Codes, a wonderful healing that works on removing stressful memories at a cellular level. Now I have recovered from the cancer I have trained in The Healing Codes as well as Reiki and both are wonderful to give as well as to receive.

I also realised that I was not alone in facing challenges after being declared NED, No Evidence of Disease. With IBC there is no 'all clear'. Hopefully time will tell whether I am one of the minority of IBC patients who live long lives with no reoccurrence.

Many women I have met have told me that that they are not the same person that they were before diagnosis; many of them wear masks, pretend to be well, smile whilst living lives of silent desperation, despair and grief for what they have lost. Because losing your old self to the disease of cancer is very similar to bereavement. You mourn for the old carefree you, the you that didn't lie awake at night wondering if the cancer will return, wondering if that twinge in your back is a sign that the cancer is marching through your body again, an unwelcome invader that shows no mercy.

According to a report in the Journal of the National Cancer Institute breast cancer survivors are 37 percent more likely to commit suicide than other women, and I am sure that there are many thousands of women living with depression and struggling alone with this.

I trained years ago in NLP, Neuro Linguistic Programming, a system for enabling change, and I am now using that experience to support women rebuilding their lives. I am very widely read in self-improvement and have trained with Anthony Robbins in goal setting and motivation. I want to pass on this knowledge, in an accessible way, to help cancer survivors move forward to happy, fulfilling lives."

Gabby explores one of the ways that adults can deal with a difficult childhood, which is a high achieving model of response. To be experiencing violence and pregnancy at 15 years old will have been emotionally challenging to say the least, but Gabby believed that she had found a way to have her 'needs' met through success at work. IBC brought with it the opportunity for her to put the brakes on, re-evaluate, re-assess and re-wire, hence her ability to understand the positivity that has come out of a massively painful and challenging experience. To go on and help others in the same situation completes the cycle and this element of the process of being 'well' is explored in Chapter Eleven.

For Chrissie it was the impact of her divorce that radically changed her entire life because she just couldn't go on with her life as it was any more.

> "I think it started when I was in the throes of separating from my ex, and I was having such a dreadful time of things at work, everything was going belly up. I was working for a company where the boss was a complete bully – I was in tears every day, and there were a number of us working there and we all felt the same. Because my relationship with my ex was breaking up I had nobody I could talk to, I was just completely a nervous wreck and I felt so alone. I remember telling a friend that my work was getting me down and she simply said 'Well, leave'. And it was almost like a realisation that it was in my control and I didn't have to put up with it.

> Like lots of people, I just got on a treadmill and I did what was expected of me and I didn't look outside that. But somebody said to me, "...this is your life and it will go where you want it to go" and in that moment, I understood that.

> I've always pretty much believed that whatever we do, we'll be fine. I've always held this belief that difficult things happen, but they will pass. I absolutely believe and know that one day three months from now, whatever the issue is today I will have forgotten about it, I'll have moved on.

I think it's that belief, that understanding that everything passes, that saw me through that time. Predominantly though, the realisation that my life *is* in my control and that I can do something about it radically changed the direction of my life.

Separating from my ex against everyone's opinions and leaving my secure, well paid job, both of which made me miserable, felt almost like a resurrection because my life had been going along a path that I wasn't happy with, that wasn't me at all. I had lost me. Over the years, I had really lost me and become someone that was just so far removed from any of my aspirations or my spirit."

What I really love about Chrissie's story is that she can pinpoint that moment that she gained the understanding with an absolute clarity that she could change her own life. How many people, I wonder, are walking around unable to realise that they have the power to make a change, to make a decision, to take a choice, even when it feels like there are no choices, or those choices feel equally despairing?

*

For me, Ann's story is really about resilience and just how much she coped with on a day to day basis, with each day bringing more and more pressure. Ann shows an enormous strength in her ability to work through each difficulty as it presents itself, in a relentless fashion.

"I'm a single parent of three children. I have two boys diagnosed with ADHD (Attention Deficit Hyperactive Disorder), one of whom also has a diagnosis of dyslexia and dyspraxia. I also have a daughter with a heart condition that developed when she was 10 years old. My eldest was diagnosed at a very young age with ADHD, at the age of five years, but we all knew well before that. Problems with him started at 13 months old, when he nearly got excluded from nursery! We had an ongoing battle from then on to try and find the cause of him not being able to walk and only run, his obstinate behaviour, aggressiveness, impulsivity and lack of attention. When he was finally diagnosed, he was classed as having severe ADHD. Then along came my daughter who was beautifully tiny with a mop of red hair. She was an actual joy in comparison to what I'd been through with my eldest. Finally along came my youngest; he was also hard work as a baby, needing constant attention or he'd scream. During the day I could not leave him alone for five minutes; even when he was asleep he would know I had left the room and wake up! He was more laid back as a toddler than my eldest; he crawled and walked rather than ran. He was about 5 when I really noticed that he did actually have the same tendencies as my eldest, but because my eldest's ADHD was so severe, I didn't recognise it earlier in my younger son. He was diagnosed at the age of 6 with ADHD but it is more like ADD

(Attention Deficit Disorder), they just don't diagnose ADD.

During this time my marriage to their dad was on the rocks. His drinking was out of control. He needed to drink every day but his personality changed with just one drink. He would come home and be very argumentative and create arguments and shove me about. I'd lost most of my friends because of the way he acted. He had very controlling behaviour.

I've always worked and studied and during the last two pregnancies I was at college and was working two part time jobs for the most of it, except during my maternity leave. I went to university for the first time when my youngest was 10 weeks old. It was in my final year that my husband and I finally separated. His constant harassment and a full time job in teaching (which I took on straight after my studies) took its toll and eventually I found myself at the doctor's suffering with depression. I had not realised I had been slowly sinking into depression which left me spending the next few months hiding in my house. I couldn't go to work, and was on sick leave for 3 months, on and off.

When I returned to work, things got worse. I had to report a colleague for sexual harassment but I requested that he was just informally warned rather than it being a formal warning. I was then singled out by the people in the department (the

Head of which was a woman) and bullied. They would not talk to me, would walk out of the room when I entered and the Head of Department started to report me for failing in the classroom. I was then investigated and constantly monitored by the Council's Education Department. I was getting good feedback from this constant observation, and I received mentoring in areas where I was a little poorer. The Education Department were good to me but this all took its toll on someone who was suffering depression and I just left in the end. This led to me failing my QTS year and my dreams of being a teacher were shot to pieces.

I worked in another sector for a few years, but then found myself being made redundant. It was during this time that I had to rush my daughter to the hospital and she was immediately sent for a brain scan. That came back clear.... I have never cried about Kristy's illness, until writing this! She was finally diagnosed with Rheumatic Fever, which affects one in a million children in this country (mainly adolescent females). It developed from a sore throat (strep A infection) and her antibodies attacked her heart and nervous system instead of her throat infection, which gave her rheumatic heart disease and Sydenham's Chorea (which was under control after 6 months and therapy). But the damage to her heart was done, affecting three of her heart valves, one severely. We came home with five different medications and a wheelchair; she was to have complete rest for 3 months. Her heart started mending and as of this year she only attends hospital for a heart scan once a year and is back to normal.

Out of all of these challenges, getting back up after the depression was the most difficult. That was 10 years ago now and I am always mindful that different people cope in different ways and some people take longer than others to recover. My strategy really is to put it behind me and start again with a deep breath and jump in!"

I shall come back to Ann in the Resilience Chapter as we explore how we can build our own resilience.

*

__Personal Ramblings__

Chapter Five – Another Place to Leave

Everyone has their own point of 'can't take it any more'.

Annett describes perfectly that sense of feeling trapped within herself, her environment and her culture.

> "I was born into a pretty rough, often violent, emotionally unavailable East German family, where I soon learned that life was tough, regimented and traumatic. So I spent most of my childhood crying, hiding and feeling deeply unhappy and frustrated. I was trapped in a crowded house and desperately wanted to get away from the intimidating behaviour, constant noise and stress. I didn't have my own personal space, so I was never able to retreat and ended up feeling constantly nervous and unsafe.
>
> Growing up in a restrictive, socialist environment also added to the picture and I found myself looking around and thinking, 'What is going on? Why is everyone so aggressive and ignorant?" Today I know it wasn't their fault. The system had limited their thinking and broken their spirit so that they had never learned to live their lives more creatively. The society was arranged on constant fear and shortage so that people would trust authority and not their intuition, thus giving their power away. Everything was designed to train humans to be like robots - brain dead automatons, like a machine that does what it is told, no

questions asked. They've tried and tested this successfully in the former East so that people were quite literary unable to think outside the box. Additionally, and perhaps like most teenagers, I didn't really know what I wanted to do with my life either, but what I did know was that I wanted to be creative, yet there were no options for me out there. I was basically born to be just another worker, to end up either in the kitchen, the factory, or the fields.

The fall of the Berlin Wall coincided with my 17th year. At first, like an animal in a cage, I was anxious to leave, but eventually this epic event that changed the lives of many inhabitants of the former GDR also served me well as a powerful generator to get me out of the limiting environment I was in.

Despite having great difficulty finding my feet, I eventually managed to travel to different places in Europe. But I was always on my own, struggling to survive and find and keep friends, including boyfriends. I was suffering terribly and by my mid-twenties I fell into the deepest depression by far. It was so bad that I cried constantly – anything would set me off. I got kicked out of jobs because I wasn't able to hold my life together. A few people tried to get me back on track, but I only saw how unloved, stupid, fat and ugly I was, unable to help myself. From my perspective I was at a dead end, ready to depart.

I had this very clear feeling that I am here, destined to be something much better, much higher and more eloquent, sophisticated, graceful, joyful and charming. I always knew how I wanted to be, I just didn't have the tools to bring that to the forefront.

In 2001, a friend suggested that I go to art college but I said, 'No, I am really not good at art. You can forget that, I have no talent or skills, I am not good at anything, I am a mess and I am definitely not an artist.' But he said, 'Go on. Try it!' So eventually I gave in and went to do a foundation course and they told me straight away that I had talent and sent me onto a degree course. It was then that I met people who encouraged me to create change within my life."

With some encouragement and open ears and a smidgeon of self-belief, Annett turned the biggest corner of her life. I love the idea that Annett would go to any lengths to find her true self, life and purpose. She left everything to find it, and find it she did. I remember that feeling of really understanding that if I was to be true to myself and if I was going to find the purpose for my existence I would do anything - absolutely anything - to get there. I wonder if it is that that is rooted in the ability to change, to seek growth and to challenge all that we know. When we do whatever we need to do to get there, even when that can be upsetting for some of those around us, and even when it feels like the hardest thing to do, then I believe we are ready for something very special to come indeed.

Rachel discovered she had dyslexia at the age of 30. It was knowledge that suddenly helped everything make sense, but within that 'making sense' process her world fell apart.

> "I hit rock bottom when I lived in Croydon. I didn't have a job because I had been made redundant and had quite a bad year of splitting up with my boyfriend. That combination, alongside failing exams, operations and car accidents, made it feel like things couldn't get any worse. It was in that context, while visiting Lincoln, that I made a snap decision that I was going to move there.
>
> Within a few months of moving to Lincoln I found out that I was severely dyslexic. I was 30 years old and I had just discovered something as important as this, which I think actually took me to rock bottom. I just felt like I had failed and been failed by those around me. I had a lot of anger towards my family and my parents for them not being able to identify that issue. I had gone through my whole life not knowing that I was dyslexic; I'd always felt something wasn't quite right but I didn't know what it was and nobody picked it up.
>
> I was very angry because my parents took on a business when I was 6 months old and they had that business until I was 16 and so most of the time in my childhood they were working in the business – they were downstairs, because we lived within the business premises. They never really spent that much time with us other than on a Sunday, which

was 'family day', but it was a *forced* family day. It had a routine, so we had to go to church at 10 o'clock and then we had to have Sunday lunch and then we had to spend the afternoon as a family and then that was your weekend over. But when we needed them they were always downstairs working. It wasn't like it was an unhappy childhood or family life, but looking back I'm very conscious that some of my issues are to do with lack of confidence and self-belief because Mum and Dad just didn't partake in my childhood. I can never remember them saying we were good at anything, or helping us with homework. It was always 'If you need us we will be downstairs.'

I found out about the dyslexia by accident really when I started studying for my nutrition qualification. My tutor back then said to me: 'I don't understand it, Rachel. Why is it that in class you are always really with it, you're really intellectual, you are bang on, but when I read your assignments it's like you're a five year old and you don't understand it?' I explained to her all the issues I was having about how what's in my head doesn't come out of my mouth, or what's in my head doesn't come out on paper how I want it to sound and I can't communicate and I have this real kind of *block* where I can't get out what I want to say in a way that I want to say it, either written or spoken. It was then that she said she thought I had dyslexia.

For £300 I could have a dyslexia test but I'd just been made redundant and I didn't have much money, so I didn't have it and then I moved to Lincolnshire. My sister is an accountant and happened to be working in an office in Nottingham shared with the Nottingham Dyslexia Association – and they happened to have an outreach programme in Lincolnshire where they were offering a test for free. The 'Quick Scan' test, which took an hour, is designed to calculate whether you have dyslexic tendencies, and if you score highly they recommend a full dyslexia test. The results really shocked me. Because it's based on children's centiles, there were some things where I came up on the 90% centile and some where I scored on the 10% centile and there's a really massive split – some things I'm really fantastic at and some things I'm really bad at.

Initially the results just really floored me. I had to learn how to love myself exactly as I was. I asked my friends what they liked about me and I took a step back and thought, actually there's a lot of people who like me for who I am and like my quirkiness and think I'm funny and think I'm hilarious and not in a condescending or bullying way, just think that because I am quite light-hearted and tend to be quite jovial. I had to learn that I've just got to accept who I am. I have a mantra: 'Live, love, laugh'. It basically means 'Live your life'.

I have this written on my bracelet and on my doormat at home and on posters. I'm always going through different things on my journey and I just think life is for living, you have to make the most of every single moment and the material things don't matter anymore. I'm just appreciative that I can look outside every morning and see the sky and it's blue. I see fields because I live in Lincolnshire and I'm thankful for the fact that Lincolnshire is beautiful and the way of life is the way of life I want to live and *things* don't matter."

I loved Rachel's enthusiasm and how she eventually chose to accept herself and be vibrant and alive whilst still ploughing through difficulties with self-esteem and confidence yet absolutely on the path of recovery and wellness.

*

Sue's journey started in the darkest of places and when I went to interview her, I had no idea about what she was going to say. I thought we were going to talk about something else entirely so I was really taken aback when she started sharing her story. Sue was quietly spoken but talked from the position of a woman who has come through huge childhood traumas that took years to recover from, leaving some scars for life.

"The story starts when I was a child and I grew up in a household where my dad was a violent bully and I was abused physically, sexually and emotionally from the age of 11 until the age of 18 when I left home. I was a bright girl at school and that always held me through life – I could see light at the end of the tunnel in the form of university - that was my beacon.

When I was 16 and taking my O Levels, as they were then, and when I was 18 taking my A Levels, my dad got sent to prison on both occasions, which left me the emotional space to get through my exams. The legacy of that childhood left me with a very deep-seated feeling that I was absolutely worthless and that I didn't matter and the core of it is that I wasn't good enough; that feeling has haunted me and been the musical accompaniment to my life. I am now 46 years old and it's only in the last three or four years that I have gradually believed, and I *do* believe now wholeheartedly, that I *am* good enough, but my journey is a series of 'staging posts' along the way and each staging post has helped me to understand and chip away at that core belief about myself.

It was at university that I met my son's dad. We were together for six years and had a child and when my son was four months old, my partner basically said 'goodbye'. He'd had an affair while I was pregnant, and I found myself a single mum when my son was four months old. Nine months before my son was born my mum died very suddenly, without warning, aged 47. She had been ill all her life and had been very much a victim of living with my dad. So my mum died, my son was born and when he was four months old I was out on my own and I just fell apart. For a good three years, maybe four years I was completely disengaged from the world around me. I would get up every morning, go to work, go through the motions, come home, look after my son, put him to bed and then there was nothing; absolutely nothing. I was having a series of relationships with *terrible* men, drinking too much to drown my sorrows and escape from my life, and when I look back now I cringe, but I was in a place where I didn't think that I mattered, and I didn't believe I was good enough and that was a particularly dark place for me.

I had those feelings from my late teens to around about the age of thirty. That's an awfully long time to have those feelings about yourself, isn't it? I was drinking too much and one day my son commented on it; he was only about 4 or 5 and I just stopped and stared and was horror-struck that at that age he could see what I was doing. It was like it took a child to point out that I was on self-destruct. At that point I just thought, 'Crikey, this isn't good, something has to change,' and I began to realise that the only person who could change anything in my life was me. It wasn't an overnight thing at all. I still continued my destructive habits, but they lessened over the years as I adopted more supportive ones."

Sue really explained her understanding of her journey through the different things that happened and how there were a number of moments, collectively pulling together a new way of living. But recovery from child abuse is widely known to take extensive personal and therapeutic work, primarily due to the extent of the damage to child development and how that will impact into adult life. I was so humbled by Sue's recovery, possibly because she is 46 years old and feels that she has only begun to 'live' in the last couple of years. While acknowledging that as a waste, she also acknowledges that it is never too late to start living and I think that is a clear, important and valuable message to everyone.

*

Personal Ramblings

Chapter Six – Revealing The Pain

"Out of suffering have emerged the strongest souls; the most massive characters are seared with scars."

Khalil Gibran

Sometimes we just don't know what life is about to throw our way, what lessons are coming, what journey we are about to embark upon, sometimes kicking and screaming. Kelly had a lovely life, a happy childhood, loving parents and was about to marry her soulmate. Cancer struck out of nowhere, as it does, and literally side swiped her and took her breath away.

> "I was diagnosed with breast cancer in 2006, when I was 31. I was diagnosed just after I'd got engaged and was planning our wedding. We were due to embark on a year-long round the world trip which was booked and paid for; we had both handed in our notice at work. We were packing our stuff, the flights were booked and four weeks before we were due to fly I was diagnosed. So I had a whole year of treatment and a mastectomy, which took me into a deep depression. All the dreams that I had had were shattered. Losing a breast, to me, was like losing my whole femininity and I had lost who I was – I'd lost my hair, and I would look in the mirror and I didn't recognise the person I'd become.
>
> While I was stuck in this depression, I wasn't really going anywhere or doing anything apart from going

to hospital appointments and internet browsing, just killing time really. I had just watched How To Look Good Naked on Channel 4 and they were asking for people to apply to go on the next series. I thought, oh I'll look at that, and you didn't have to be interviewed or auditioned or queue up, you just had to fill in an online form. The questions were quite thought provoking, so I started filling some of them out and even at that stage I didn't know whether I would actually send it off, but it was quite therapeutic in its own right just to write it down and send it off, and I was chosen to take part.

They picked seven ladies out of 10,000 applications for my series. It takes quite a few months to go through the selection process, but one of the questions they asked me was designed to sift out the people who just want to be friends with Gok. They asked me: 'If you were picked do you think you could do this? Do you think you could do what is required of the show?' and I said, 'I don't know whether I could' and they pretty much said that was the right answer.

People said 'Oh you are really brave to do that, I wouldn't have the confidence to take my clothes off on the telly' but for me it was the opposite. I felt so low that I felt I had nothing to lose; it wasn't somebody who had a normal frame of mind where it could be humiliating. For me I couldn't feel worse than I already did and people couldn't think any less of me. To me, somebody who is not really a risk taker in life, it was a risk worth taking.

They fitted me in a wedding dress that you couldn't wear a bra underneath and this very lovely fashion lady called Jane would dress me. What you see on the telly is authentic, it's real, you see a reaction in the mirror when you see those clothes for the first time, what you're seeing is real and they achieve that by dressing you blindfolded, so I had to have lots of wedding dress fittings blindfolded. For the last fitting Jane couldn't come and I went with a very beautiful, very slim, very tall 24 year old researcher called Laura, who hadn't seen mastectomy scars before, and I think actually she was more petrified than I was. When I undressed, she said to me 'Your scar is beautiful' and I cried and she cried and that moment will stay with me forever – people don't judge you the way you judge yourself... Moments like that, which you don't see on the TV, really changed how I felt about myself.

Gok really challenged me about how I felt about myself and there were some real humdingers! One involved me throwing my handbag on the floor in an Oxford Street store and Gok running down Oxford Street after me - you draw a crowd when you're being chased by Gok Wan! And at one point he shouted at me and said 'If you don't change how you think about yourself, I can't help you' and that is so true, he helped me change how I felt about myself. Yes, they did my hair, they did my make-up, they gave me nice clothes, but that programme completely changed my life and it wasn't because of hair and make-up or clothes, it was because they challenged how I thought about myself."

I think Kelly describes so well a completely unforeseen journey of self-discovery, not only dealing with the shock of breast cancer at such a young age, but also the shock of recovery and what it gave her. She articulates how, ultimately, it has little to do with how you look on the outside but everything to do with your relationship with yourself and how you feel on the inside. The circumstances that Kelly had to explore this within are visually challenging for a young woman in her prime, to say the least, and I can only imagine what it must have felt like at the beginning of that process.

*

Sarah talks about how her experiences over the last eight years have given her the strength she needs to carry on making sense of being 'ordinary' dealing with 'extraordinary'. When life happens, when your world is upended through someone else's choices or an accident or ill health, it can be really difficult to manage emotionally and practically.

"We generally change ourselves for one of two reasons: inspiration or desperation." Jim Rohn

"Eight years ago I had what I now realise was a pretty good life. I now really understand the old cliché, you don't know what you've got until it's gone!

I was in my late 30s and I had been back in the UK for a couple of years. I'd just bought my first property in London and I had a good job. I enjoyed my sport and had hobbies and an active social life. I'd travelled and worked and competed in my sport overseas and had friends across the globe spanning America and Australia through to Israel and Africa.

I'm not saying I was in a state of complete happiness and fulfilment. Why would I be? Our whole western civilisation dictates we must find our soul mate, start a family and seek personal fulfilment through all of these things. It's not that I really bought into that idea but I do think, like all of us, I was influenced by it. I thought I could have my happily ever after and I had a good idea of what I thought that looked like.

Eight years later and my vision of happily ever after could not be more different. I have learnt to live in the day and take each day as it comes and so I therefore don't have a vision of happily ever after anymore.

Everything was about to change when I met the man I married. He was lovely and together we planned to have a baby. All my friends and family liked him and I liked all of his friends and family. He had a good business and older children from a previous relationship that he remained involved with. He was kind and generous and funny and capable and we were happy. Everything changed in a flash when, what seemed like out of the blue, he had a mental breakdown. This culminated in him going out for a run shortly after our daughter was born and not coming back for months. When he did return we really tried to be together but over the course of that following year he went missing many times.

I devoured books about depression and I became a fully paid up member of the emotional distance club. I started to separate myself from everything around me and I stepped out of his slipstream. I learnt to have a Plan B activity for my baby daughter and me in case everything had to change at the last minute. My emotional wellbeing and, by association, that of my child, was dependent on me not falling apart with disappointment and resentment. Saying that this wasn't easy is putting it lightly.

During all that turmoil, shortly after my daughter turned three years old, my brother fell down some stairs, sustaining a massive head injury, and was rushed into theatre for life saving surgery. My whole family - my mum and step dad, me and my daughter and my brother's two teenage children, to whom he was a single parent - huddled at the hospital playing the waiting game.

The next few days were a blur. Would he survive? How damaged would his brain be? We spent hours in ICU holding his hand, willing him to squeeze or blink. He was ventilated, in a coma with enormous bandages around his head. They were long, long hours filled with dread interspersed with calls to my sister in Australia and to my brother's friends.

I'd wake in the night visualising his funeral before banishing those thoughts and actively trying to visualise his recovery. I started with the big stuff - total and complete recovery. After a week or two I was down to the flicker of an eyelid or the raising of a little finger.

Eventually he came round but there were no miraculous first words or actions to reassure us that he would be fine. He was moved into high dependency and he progressed slowly from writing to speaking. He was able to eat, he didn't especially seem to know who we were but he did know our names. He was able to walk with the aid of nurses.

As it became apparent that his recovery would be limited and a long time coming we decided his children should come to live with me. At 17 and 15 they were very resistant to leaving their city home and moving a little further out into the suburbs.

I went from single mum of a toddler, pretty much independent and doing my own thing with a loving mother and stepfather supporting me, to suddenly becoming a full time guardian to two teens who were facing the hardest experience of their lives. They'd only ever known me as an auntie on family weekends and occasional family holidays, sender of (usually late) birthday cards with money in them. Previously, my parents had hosted Sunday lunch and special occasion meals, helped out with childcare and treated us to trips out and about. All of a sudden we were thrust together into overwhelmingly close quarters, topped off with the desperate worry for our son/dad/uncle/brother's health and wellbeing.

For me in my early/mid 40s, for my parents in their 70s, for my niece and nephew in their teens, negotiating this minefield of emotion, responsibility, relationships and re-making ourselves into a functioning unit has been one of the hardest things my family has faced.

The very reason I wanted to be involved in this book is because I believe myself to be an ordinary woman. I've dealt with the extraordinary things that have happened to me in an ordinary way.

Through these events I had my rock bottom. Not all in one go, not dramatically, not in a light bulb moment. But through all of this I have learnt, and continue to learn, many things. I have needed a desire to be pro-active and I'm guessing you have that desire already if you're reading this. For me there was a pivotal point at which I chose to stop reacting. There was a point at which I felt a consciousness beginning to re-assert itself and that's when I started making decisions rather than having them 'done' to me.

Another part of that turning point, ironically and slightly paradoxically, was gaining an acceptance of my situation. That acceptance hasn't meant a passive surrender. Acceptance for me was to put an end to 'being done to' and to start 'doing for myself'. Acceptance doesn't stop the universe throwing you curve balls; it just leaves you more heart and soul to field those balls.

Acceptance allowed me to stop wasting my energy on futile regrets and what ifs. It helped me let go of a lot of the anger that was exhausting me. Railing against the unfairness of it all insidiously worked to reinforce my feelings of helplessness.

I arrived at acceptance exhausted by fighting what I could not change. Conversely, giving up that fight gave me clarity and the energy to focus on the things I could change."

Sarah's story shows how change can come in different forms and shapes. Rather than the 'light bulb' moment Chrissie had, realising she could live a different life, Sarah's realisation was one of internal strength and empowerment.

For Sarah, none of her circumstances could be changed; she couldn't run away from her responsibility as a mother any more than she could turn her back on her brother's children, but she had to change something. The way she viewed her circumstances and the impact that it had on her life had to be different. Sarah's process of change was not that she could make her external circumstances different, but she learnt that she could make the way she reacted to them different.

How we see and react to our situation is as powerful in dealing with it as is changing that which makes us unhappy or feel unfulfilled. Sometimes we're just not able to change a situation at that point in our lives, but it is the way we react that will bring us the internal shift that we need to go on. I love how Sarah brings this to life in her story and how, in changing her view of what life has brought her, she has achieved a peace within herself which has enabled her to do what she knows to be the best thing to do while building the resilience to deal with it.

*

Amy describes how she has dealt with becoming a carer for her father while going through the process of growing up and dealing with some of life's challenges.

> "In 2001 I returned from my first year at university a new person. Or so I thought. I was naïve to think that I would do all my growing up there and in the early years of my 20s. I didn't consider that you are constantly growing up, it doesn't just happen, and it takes a lot of time!
>
> When I returned from university everything was pretty much perfect. Mum and Dad owned their

own company running barge holidays throughout Europe. As far as I was concerned it had given them a new lease of life, doing something completely different. Secretly I was proud, but would never have told them at the time. That first summer back home we all noticed that Dad was having trouble breathing. Mum said it had been going on for a few months but it took us until Christmas that same year to persuade him to go to the doctor's. We thought perhaps asthma or some kind of heart problem. The doctor couldn't find anything and I think just told Dad to walk the dog a bit more often, which he did. Then in the spring of the following year Dad developed a stutter; coincidentally it started just after his Dad died – we thought perhaps it was down to stress – you never know and are never in control of how your body reacts to grief. My life was starting to get stressful too. I had returned home (tail between my legs) after having split from my fiancé. Six months later I found out that he had been cheating on me with one of his work colleagues; they had been together for a year, been together while he and I planned our wedding, taken our dogs out for a walk together and slept together in our bed. You can imagine that, at the age of 22, this was a rather major event in my life! But who did I turn to? Family, of course. I found a tremendous amount of strength in them. It took me a long time to find myself after that – it was this time of my life when I discovered Reiki and the mantra that would remain with me to this day: Fake it till you make it. My Reiki teacher taught me to visualise certain situations. I had totally lost my confidence and self-belief - Reiki pretty much saved my life. I still go to the same Reiki teacher today and since then she has saved my life many times.

We noticed that Dad started falling nearly every day and his speech was deteriorating month by month. Finally, after he was misdiagnosed with Parkinson's and other related degenerative illnesses, he decided to have a private brain scan. The result: Progressive Supranuclear Palsy. We were told that there is hardly any information out there on this terminal brain disease; we were only handed a leaflet and told that it is what Dudley Moore had. Our family have always been close, I was so proud of the fact that we got on so well, we actually liked each other! My sister and I had such a laugh with Mum and Dad and growing up (apart from a few disastrous teenage years) we were all friends. Over a period of around five years Dad has deteriorated reasonably slowly, although as of today I would say within the last year there has been a rapid decline. His speech has been reduced to one word answers if we are lucky, normally just a nod or shake of the head,; he is unable to walk unaided; we have to mash up all his food and feed him; we have to take him to the toilet and help him wash.

In 2010 I decided to give up my 9-5 events co-ordinator job and care for Dad full time. To me, there was no other option. On a selfish note, I felt that I needed to spend more time with him; I didn't want to miss the opportunity and look back with regret. Looking after a loved one who has a terminal illness is not for everyone and I am constantly asked how I do it. My answer - I do it because I have to – in my view, he looked after me for pretty much 25 years so it is the least I can do. We were thick as thieves once; we are now too but it's very different. As much as it is rewarding, knowing that this is what he wants, he doesn't want a stranger looking after him, he wants me.

At the same time, my sister, my Mum and I decided to open a shop. We don't do things by halves in our family. I now believe that if you can dream it, you can do it! Mum has always been creative; she is one of those people who can turn their hand to pretty much anything, but we never thought that it would be Dad's illness that would bring out the creative side of us all. She had been making handbags and selling them at craft markets; my sister was making jewellery and selling them with Mum pretty much every Saturday, come rain or shine. It was a cold, rainy and windy day when Mum suddenly said: 'Why don't we open our own shop?!' My sister and I went along with it, viewing property, looking into the legal side etc. Within three weeks we had secured a property and had started painting and decorating.

We called the shop The Blue Room. The idea was that we would sell only handmade, locally produced things created by local people. On the open day we had eight other artists involved - painters, jewellery makers, ceramicists and photographers, to name but a few. Two years later we have 40 artists involved and we have already moved to bigger premises. We changed our outlook on life quite quickly after Dad was diagnosed with PSP – when you are faced with a terminal illness, you do tend to evaluate your life and put all aspects of it under the microscope. You realise that dreams are really meant to become reality and actually if you achieve them you set yourself aside from the rest.

We figured out that once you have achieved one dream there is nothing stopping you – we had to have this positivity in our lives to counteract the utter sadness and realisation that we were losing Dad.

We needed to become a lot more flexible and at first I struggled to break free of the conventional 9-5 boundaries. I was able to spend more time with Dad while Mum concentrated on the daily running of The Blue Room. I focused all my efforts on making Dad as comfortable, safe and happy as I possibly could. I also started working on a childhood dream - writing and publishing children's books. I had had this idea for years, and woke up one morning thinking 'Come on Amy, just do it – stop thinking about it and do it!' So I did. It was the hardest thing I have ever done in my life - and also the most rewarding. Telling Dad about the reviews as they came in was just amazing; seeing his face made it all worthwhile. He may not have been able to say it but in his eyes I knew he was proud.

We learnt very quickly how hard it is to be a carer – Mum, Nicola and I promised Dad that we would keep him at home for as long as possible though it was something we had to fight the NHS and local authorities for. It would have been a lot easier for us to put him in a home and try to get on with our lives, but we made a promise to an amazing man who probably doesn't even know how much of an effect he has had on our lives.

Throughout Dad's illness we have faced battles for the simplest things: funding, facilities, dignity and equipment. It can't just be us that face this struggle on a daily basis? This is why we wanted to offer free workshops for carers at The Blue Room – we understand the need for time alone or indeed time doing something creative. We have recently started to get this project off the ground with the help of some volunteers. We decided to make The Blue Room a Community Interest Company in the autumn last year so that we could give something positive back to the community. The Blue Room has evolved so much over the past two years and has become a real lifeline for us. We offer work experience to local students, we sponsor an art student at the local college and we offer free spaces on our workshops for carers. We hope that this will make a difference, even if it is small, to a carer's life.

I would say to anyone in our situation: You may have to fight for what you want so arm yourselves with everything you can lay your hands on, make notes about *everything*, take whatever support is out there, counselling, Reiki, talk to people, try not to shut people out, but also - you are stronger than you think. It's natural for you to re-evaluate your life when faced with a terminal illness so if there is something you have always wanted to do, now is the time to do it - or at least start to plan! Go for it! The Blue Room has been a godsend (although the hard work has been entirely down to us) for Mum; it's somewhere she can go where no one knows about Dad. It's a calm and relaxing place where people love to be – they love to browse, slow shop, take their time and have a chat about all the beautiful things we have in the shop. Seeing the people loving the courses they are taking part in is so rewarding. I'm so proud that out of a terrible situation we have made a positive impact on people's lives, including our own."

The important message here that bounds through is about how there are some things that we just cannot change. What we can change are our attitudes, view and understanding. The power lies right there.

*

"God grant me the serenity, to accept the things I cannot change, the courage to change the things I can and the wisdom to know the difference."

The Serenity Prayer

*

Personal Ramblings

Chapter Seven – Overcoming Adversity

When I first started to think about the women I wanted to be involved in this book, I specifically asked for women who had 'overcome adversity', who had dealt with something major that really impacted upon their lives, that they had learnt from, grown from, thrived and prospered from in some way.

So what is adversity?

ad·ver·si·ty [ad-vur-si-tee] noun, plural ad·ver·si·ties

1. Adverse fortune or fate; a condition marked by misfortune, calamity, or distress: A friend will show his or her true colours in times of adversity.

2. An adverse or unfortunate event or circumstance: You will meet many adversities in life.

Origin:
1200–50; Middle English adversite (< Anglo-French) < Latin adversitās. See adverse, -ity

Synonyms
1. catastrophe, disaster; trouble, misery. 2. See affliction.

Antonyms
1. prosperity.

*

We have explored a variety of stories and there are more to come that take us on different journeys and through different types of adversity, looking at the ongoing process of moving on and how that manifests in a positive way.

However, I wanted to recognise that adversity is a daily experience for some of us. It is not something that comes from nowhere but is a part of life - but seeking change within that is very possible.

Rani's story explores this so well while also demonstrating the impact that consciousness and awareness can have on social change.

> "I'm 3rd generation British Asian, British Indian and was born in Birmingham. My mother had a disability; she had a glass eye. She came to this country married to my father, who was 14 years senior to her, and with four very grown up step-children. I was born into a 'typical' Indian household and the discussions were always political, but my mother was fairly young when she got married to my dad. I remember my first memories were of quite a stern father, and I witnessed domestic violence towards my mother.
>
> As a child, the impact that that had on me was huge. Since then it's very much that my 'story' has been about justice and fairness to all, regardless of what background people have come from. Unfortunately my father died when I was six years old and my mother was left with 4 stepchildren and 2 of her own. My brother was only 6 months old so my mother had her hands full.
>
> The challenges that I watched my mother face were paramount to the development of my integrity now

as Rani, who I am, and my beliefs about fairness, justice and the inequalities that prevail in all societies.

Growing up in an Indian society, I observed Mum being discriminated against because she had a glass eye. She had had to marry my father, who was so much older than her and already had children, because nobody else would ever marry her because of her glass eye, her 'disability'. So there were already challenges when she arrived in a country where she didn't know anyone and couldn't speak English, and they were very big mountains to climb.

My sense of unfairness developed at a young age in the context of being brought up without a father in a Sikh community which was, and still is to a certain degree, *very* patriarchal, and I saw my mother battle through all those challenges, with all of the associated discrimination.

When I got married and moved from Birmingham to Slough I also felt the isolation, even though I understood how the system 'worked' - the police, education and so on. I realised that isolation can be felt by anyone, it doesn't matter what your socio-economic background is, or your faith or your education, it can be anyone at any given time. This was my reason for starting my charity, Jeena. Jeena means 'to live' and our motto is 'challenging social norms' because that is what I do. Both as a community activist and as a mother or a friend, I will challenge whatever norms there are, whether they're based on culture or faith.

When my daughter was born there was a lot of doom and gloom around giving birth to a girl. When my second daughter was born I actually had people phoning up saying 'I'm really sorry, God will prevail!' and I was thinking, this is not right. We are all women, you know, where is the 'sisterhood'?

So for me, adversity has been an ongoing experience rather than one thing that happened to me. Rani being a little girl, Rani being a teenager, Rani getting married, Rani being a mother, Rani being a sister – throughout my life there has been adversity.

This has usually been because of gender bias actually, which I think is prevalent in a lot of communities and in society as a whole. One of the first films we made when I started the charity is called 'From the beginning' and its focus is about gender inequalities within the Asian community specifically, but it affects all communities. Women travel from this country, from Britain, to go to India and have self-selecting abortions because they want boys; so they are aborting female foetuses.

So for me that is what Jeena is all about - challenging social norms, whether it's about honour based violence, forced marriages, whether it's to do with the challenges within yourself – 'I can't do this because I'm not educated, I haven't got a degree'. I just about passed my A-levels, so it doesn't matter what education background you are from. I think often our worst challenge is the enemy within. 'It's because I'm a woman, it's because I'm not educated, it's because I haven't got money, I've got children'. I've got all those things, I've got five children, but it doesn't stop me from leading what I hope is a productive life and making a difference to an individual."

Fuelled by her passion and drive for fairness and equality, Rani throws herself into her charity work, and continues to face all sorts of obstacles. I asked her to explore this.

"Knowing yourself and what you are all about and then believing in yourself is a good start. Of course there are days when my glass is half empty, but most days my glass is half full and that's really important. Money is a big issue in my life. I live in a council house, I have nothing in my house - we haven't even got carpets! But I am happy because I've got a roof over my head, I've got five beautiful children who are healthy and money comes and goes, so to me it will happen and I have got that belief that it will happen; it's happening now with the way that things are going. Two years now I have dedicated to my charity and I've not been paid a penny, but the belief is that it will happen and money isn't everything; it helps, but it's not everything. It's being in that right place.

Never ever think that you can do it alone, there is always someone or something that will actually help you to deal with whatever it may be. And aim higher. I never ever thought that I would have an invitation from the Houses of Parliament. And this is little old me, a housewife with five children living in Slough, and I'm thinking, Wow! You know. So always strive to be the best you possibly can - and if you can think it, you can be it."

*

Judith spoke to me about how she became psychotic in her thirties. She has written her own book about this terrifying experience in which she seeks to break down the walls of silence and the shame and stigma around mental health.

"The phone rang and I screamed. I was filled with terror. My heart began to pound and I started to shake. In my confused mind I had become the deaf, dumb and blind boy in *Tommy*, a film that had captivated me many years before. I moved my limbs in a stilted and robotic way. I was no longer myself. I was in a different world, the world of psychosis. I was trapped and could not find my way out.

Becoming psychotic in my thirties has been the most terrifying experience of my life. The hallucinations were horribly frightening and I found myself almost frozen with fear and panic. I struggled constantly to understand what was happening to me.

I'd grown up in a dysfunctional family and became depressed in my teens, following the death of my grandmother. I went on to marry an abusive man who was a bully and a sexual pervert. My marriage was as dysfunctional as my upbringing and family life had been and I experienced rape and domestic violence for over three years before I found the courage to leave. After four weeks of sick leave and tears, I threw myself into my work and tried to forget. Bottling up my emotions made me more and more anxious. I gradually deteriorated and became psychotic.

I was taken to the psychiatric hospital and for the first eleven days I refused all food and drink, believing I was dead. I was sectioned under the Mental Health Act - to save my life rather than my sanity - and spent six months in hospital. I was heavily medicated and had six treatments of electro convulsive therapy (ECT) – a barbaric practice which gave me the worst headaches ever, but the treatments did bring me back to reality.

Coming home from hospital was overwhelming and I felt small, helpless, lost and alone. I'd been medically retired from my civil service job and felt physically weak from all the months of inactivity in hospital and I remember my GP telling me to go walking to build up my leg muscles. My confidence had gone, my motivation had gone and I needed to start again. I didn't know where to start initially. Some days I had to take it hour by hour and my progress was slow until I built up a routine and started to go out and to join classes, do voluntary work and feel more confident around people. I was still taking anti-depressant and anti-psychotic medication but it started to dawn on me that change was possible and I could manage without medication and eventually I was able to cut down and finally come off all the tablets.

My life changed from monochrome to full colour, my feelings returned and I started to dream again. A friend said I was 'all lit up'. After the years of darkness I started to live properly again. I met Ken, who was loving and supportive, totally the opposite of my first partner, and Ken and I married after a year. Having such a supportive partner has been very important for me; to have that support has helped so much."

I can't imagine that the impact of such of an experience would ever leave a person. However, Judith has since written about her experience with the specific purpose of working through her own healing, and she hopes her book will help others make sense of their own mental health issues.

A diagnosis of depression at the age of 22 must be such a shock. But Jayne had just that, on the back of a childhood of feeling 'less than' and with family members also experiencing different mental health issues.

"For as long as I can remember there has always been a nagging voice in my head telling me that I'm not good enough and I can do better.

Until I was 22, it was pretty easy to ignore and I suppose I was very lucky in that I sailed through life in a whirlwind of bubbly, extroverted, social butterfly-type behaviour – doing well at school, having a close knit family and a wide circle of friends.

In 2004, at the age of 22, life as I knew it came to a halt.

It was at this time I was diagnosed with depression. I didn't really know much about depression even though my sister had it. All I knew about the illness at that time was from my experience of my sister's depression, which wasn't much as she had withdrawn into herself and seemed angry at the world, including me. To be honest, it frightened me and rather than try to understand, I let my sister withdraw away from me. I also knew that my granddad had a nervous breakdown before I was born and received electric shock therapy.

Needless to say, all things mental health scared me and that's how I felt when I was diagnosed – frightened, ashamed, panicked, anxious and I had the overwhelming urge to run away from everything and everyone.

Researching depression online only made matters worse as I read story after story about people who harmed themselves, committed suicide and the words bonkers, insane bandied about.

To say I isolated myself is an understatement. I felt I couldn't but also didn't want to tell anyone. I became the master of telling white lies about why I couldn't attend this function, why I was losing weight (a side effect of the medication I had started taking) and why I wasn't answering my phone. In fact, answering my phone is the one thing I have yet to conquer. My depression made me fearful of the phone ringing. I think it was because I was worried someone would want something from me and I wouldn't be able to deliver and also because telling white lies is exhausting and made me feel even more ashamed of who I'd become.

Losing my job in 2005 was the beginning of it all going really bad for me. I was too ashamed to tell my employer why I was underperforming at work; I was signed off for long periods at a time and ended up just not returning to that job.

With hindsight, and knowing what I know now, I could have done so much more to remain in employment. I also know that being employed gave me a reason to get up in the morning, get dressed and leave the house. Without it, things soon took a downhill dive for me. I stopped washing, stopped seeing anyone if I could help it, ate little, slept lots and couldn't bear to see myself in the mirror.

During this time my boyfriend Dom proposed to me and we got married. He was a childhood sweetheart so I knew I loved him and that, well or not well, it was the right decision. It baffles me that he still wanted to marry me though; I wasn't exactly a catch at this point but the fact that he loved me despite all of this and showed such courage, strength and patience means that I knew that when we said 'for better, for worse' in our vows, it was said with conviction.

I don't remember the exact 'turning point' when it all changed for me but I do know that coming off anti-depressants was the best thing I ever did. That sentence coming after what you've just read probably sounds a bit crazy but I just couldn't find the right medication. The first one I tried stopped me from sleeping at all and led to dramatic weight loss whilst the second one just made me angry, and anyone who knows me knows I've not ever really been an angry person.

So in 2010 I came off my medication and spent days online reading about what I could do to help myself. At this point I was working as a self-employed bookkeeper with Dom. It worked well for us because we could work from home and work hours which suited us.

The information I gathered seemed to boil down to two things – nutrition and exercise. I was still very anxious about leaving the house at this point so put exercise on hold whilst I tried to sort my diet. Depression always takes away my appetite or makes me crave junk food so changing my eating habits was hard. I started by taking a multi-vitamin and mineral supplement every day. Then I gradually introduced more fruit, vegetables, whole grains, avoided fizzy drink, avoided alcohol and tried my best to limit junk food intake. It did help, it wasn't a miracle fix but it did give me energy, my skin started looking less grey and my nails started growing faster than I knew what to do with them. It also made me wonder what exercise might do for me and gradually, with Dom's help, I managed to leave the house and go walking, often miles at a time, and it felt good. I was still an easy crier but I was starting to smile again.

Towards the end of 2010, Mum bought me a journal and I started writing in it every morning. This awakened in me the love of writing which I'd forgotten I even enjoyed. This then led onto a blog in which I was open about my depression for the first time. To say that was empowering was an understatement. There I was, talking about the illness which had robbed me of the best part of my twenties and I was not only being accepted for it but congratulated and thanked for being honest. Well, once I'd started it was like a dam had burst and I couldn't stop. It was great to be me, warts and all and for people to accept that.

This was a real turning point and I started to realise that whilst the old Jayne was probably never going to come back, I could maybe draw on my experiences and almost create a new, improved self. I'd lost track of who I really was so started making lists of things I thought I might enjoy and doing them. I made a scrapbook of outfits I liked from magazines and bought them. I was starting to find my identity but had an overwhelming urge to help people.

One of the blog posts I'd written was about stigma – how it had affected me and how in my opinion it destroys relationships and lives. I received such a response, I was overwhelmed and my inbox was full of people who could relate to my post.

This set off a firework of thoughts in my head. I decided that I wanted to help people who were struggling with depression. Not just those who had it but also those who are affected because they love, like, live with someone with depression. When I was ill, the GP had suggested a support group but as leaving the house was such a battle it was a no-go for me so I thought I'd come up with one online - and Blurt was born.

Blurt properly launched in August 2011 and has given me a new lease of life because I am doing something worthwhile. We have already helped over 500 people and hope to help thousands more. I do have to be careful as I have learnt that I am very much an all or nothing kinda gal and when I have the bit between my teeth, I tend to roll with it until I crumple in a heap of exhaustion. It's a learning curve and I'm still very much learning about myself. For example, I never knew I was so ambitious, that I was so creative and that I had such a longing to travel. Whilst I can't get those eight years back, I am trying to not dwell on it. Some days I beat myself up as I feel I wasted those years but I have to remind myself depression is an illness, not a weakness.

I still have the nagging voice in my head, it's nowhere near as strong as it was when I was really ill and I tend to ignore it and carry on regardless. I have learnt that it is important to be as kind to yourself as you are to others and also that others want to help, you just have to let them.

I do still have bad days/weeks but the Chinese proverb 'without wind there would be no waves' reminds me that it's OK, they'll pass."

One of the messages I want to get across is about the complexity of change. There were so many routes that this book could have taken: the psychology of change, the politics of change, societal change, individual's ability to change. Essentially I just wanted to share real people's stories to demonstrate the complexity of the human condition in dealing with adversity, tackling change, recovering, healing and ultimately how people live 'successfully' when life has hit them hard.

We need to recognise that we do not live in isolation; we live in a society filled with people, places, systems, policies, beliefs, etc. I have seen so many books and messages about how *all* change comes from within. In this context, we are only individuals living alone on little islands. If this is the case, then no one has any responsibility for their communities, their families, for each other. And then, of course, what happens to the people who cannot, for whatever reason, make that change? Are they not to be helped, supported and loved?

I would argue that while it is the case that it matters how we as individuals respond and react and manage and deal with the world we live in, it is not the end of the story.

I am indeed saying that we have a responsibility and an ability to make a difference to ourselves from within, using the tools that are featured throughout the book. Our internal space requires growth and nurture and that is our very own personal responsibility. However, where we can, we have to strive to ensure that the social structures in place are designed to help us live in a fair society; a society that seeks to ensure justice and an understanding about the real experiences for people living, not only in our society, but all around the world. All is not equal and fair and we are absolutely not 'all in this together'.

And finally, what I also believe with all my heart, knowledge and experience is that collaboration at all levels of our being is vital to secure individual change, social change and ultimately global change. We have to work together, supporting each other, and nurturing each other so that we can grow as individuals and then make an impact upon our communities and beyond.

Definition of COLLABORATE; intransitive verb

> 1: to work jointly with others or together, especially in an intellectual endeavour

> 2: to cooperate with or willingly assist an enemy of one's country and especially an occupying force

> 3: to cooperate with an agency or instrumentality with which one is not immediately connected

I have always tried to work collaboratively and it has become a way of life for me now in just about every area. Naturally thriving in communities, we can only build so much on our own. As women, it is our natural habitat to work together, build together, parent our children together and grow together.

To me it feels like this natural collaboration has been lost in society for a good few decades, but now we have the Internet and social media - tools to let us collaborate in groups (think Facebook), in circles (think Google), in chat rooms, in pictures (think Pinterest), with people all over the world. We need to work together for our own individual development, to improve our communities and make them sustainable and to create social change to make sure that our children's children live in a world that we find acceptable, at the very least - though I pledge that I will fight for more than that!

__Personal Ramblings__

Chapter Eight – Understanding and Letting Go of Shame

"Until you make the unconscious conscious, it will direct your life and you will call it fate."- C.G. Jung

Through the stories told here, shame has come up over and over again. Feeling trapped with a deep sense of isolation and despair, clinging tightly to the belief that no one else has been through this or has felt this or feels as bad as you feel or that you are a bad person (because you absolutely must be bad for these things to happen) has been a recurring theme.

The difference between guilt and shame is that guilt is borne out of something you have done and can therefore by definition be something you can repair. Shame is the feeling or emotion you can have when something has been done *to* you, for example an abuse. Shame renders you powerless, leaving the person abused feeling unable to change it.

What has undoubtedly given people a key from which to escape this box of suffocation was finding other people to connect with, to discover positive examples of openness about things such as child abuse, addiction etc. It is this factor - the acknowledgement that we are not alone, which then breaks the chains that have previously prevented healing.

Many years ago, at the beginning of my recovery from alcoholism, I found a book and some tapes (it was long before the age of podcasts, downloads and iPods!) by John Bradshaw. I listened to him talk about what he calls 'Toxic

Shame' and his description of how this causes anxiety and depression and prevents a healthy development of self-esteem and an ability to be connected to other human beings, as long as it is left to thrive. Toxic shame is not the same as healthy shame, which keeps us from behaving in ways that are detrimental to our self-esteem. Toxic shame is unhealthy shame that further damages the damaged. This kind of shame is deeply isolating and feeds a sense of aloneness in the deepest possible way. I really connected with this.

"To be shame-bound means that whenever you feel any feeling, need or drive, you immediately feel ashamed. The dynamic core of your human life is grounded in your feelings, needs and drives. When these are bound by shame, you are shamed to the core."[5]

Interestingly, even though I spent a lot of time in early recovery working through shame, starting the development of self-love and a spiritual belief that enabled me to make that initial break from the internal entrapment I suffered, I very rarely spoke about having been a child in care or a homeless teenager across the 18 or so years that I worked in education and in Social Services with young people who were in care or were escaping homelessness. In that setting I found the 'them' and 'us' culture to be rife; an irony indeed. I remember being on multi-disciplinary child protection courses along with social workers, teachers, police, psychiatric nurses, doctors, to name but a

---

[5] *Healing the Shame that Binds You* John Bradshaw

few. Through listening to the language they used and the recounting of 'cases' they worked with, I knew that they saw no connection between themselves and the people that they were being paid to 'assist', support and help. I hated every moment of it and had to silence my internal dialogue about what I was observing, all the while knowing that I was not 'us' but I wasn't 'them' either.

I understand now that I, on some level, still felt ashamed about what had happened to me because essentially I felt I would be judged or even worse, rendered 'special' or patronised by being given the illusion of a voice. A series of incidents over many years took me to the point where I wanted to shout about what had happened to me. On one particular occasion at a dinner party at a friend's large Cotswolds cottage I listened to people continuously vilifying the homeless. It eventually led to me having an outburst about whether the person concerned thought that *I* was worthy of helping or not, given that my middle class(ish) lifestyle reflected something as far removed from someone experiencing homelessness as you can find.

In the early part of the 1990s while I was studying, I earned some money working in residential homes and children's homes. I remember having a heart to heart with the manager one shift. For whatever reason, I told him that I had been in care and he replied, "I always find children who have been in care are very angry." I found this to be interestingly unhelpful and fuelled by judgement.

Another really big eye opener for me was handed to me on a plate, when I applied for a job in around 2003 for a charity that worked with people across the country who were looked after by the local authority in a setting of advocacy. There were four intense stages of interview and I got the job over 200 people. I didn't take it. They had specified they didn't want anyone with a care background. I had made my point, albeit only internally to myself.

In the settings in which I worked I understood clearly that I would be judged, so I told very few people and just busied myself when colleagues talked about their comfortable family experiences, many of which they took for granted as being the norm. It was easy to blend into the background they believed I had because they saw me through their own lens and life experience. I certainly didn't tell people about the homelessness or the recovery from alcoholism unless I was absolutely certain that they could deal with it, and I never shared details. It was often a cold, emotionless, blanket statement without the details.

It is important that we understand the interconnection between how society sees the challenges that individuals face and then, of course, how we internalise that ourselves. Take the example of Childline[6], a relentless, well publicised media campaign that put the words 'child abuse' on the tables of British homes like nothing had before. In this area, some progress has been made but that does not detract from the deep shame and consequential damage that an individual is likely to carry after

---

[6] Childline was established and launched in 1986 by Esther Rantzen and has since counselled over one million children and young people. www.childline.org.uk

experiencing abuse. However, since the launch of Childline there are far more opportunities to make the unconscious conscious, which then helps the process of removing shame begin.

What I have also learnt is that there are some social stigmas that are also judged socially. For example, addiction and homelessness have evoked some of the most judgemental and dehumanising comments I have heard. Both of these states are particularly vilified because the belief is that you have done this to yourself, unlike something like cancer or child abuse which has been done to you. The anomaly in this observation, however, is mental health, which still carries a pained stigma and judgement noted primarily but not exclusively in the way the media broaches complex mental health issues. There is often a suspicion towards people and a fear which feeds negative attitudes and, I suspect, can hinder any recovery. Time To Change[7] is a campaign that acknowledges that one in four of us will experience a mental health problem and therefore actively seeks to tackle the stigma, attitudes and behaviour towards this issue.

In this regard, it is a complete impossibility for us to separate ourselves from the society in which we live. We are social beings surrounded by social structures that inform how we respond to certain things and how those

---

[7] Time To Change is a charity led by Mind and Rethink Mental Illness, created in 2008 as an attempt to end the stigma and discrimination that face people with mental health problems. www.time-to-change.org.uk

around us react to them. We are 'told' what is acceptable and what is not, what we can publicly cry about and what we cannot. When the nation wept over the death of Diana, whose pain was that for which they sobbed? Diana? Her children? The Royal Family? When the public found out how she coped with infidelity and her isolation and an eating disorder, the tears followed en masse and public view shifted into a kinder space, particularly around anorexia. What I'm clarifying here is that there is a direct link between society and the individual in all aspects, but for the purposes of this discussion, the aspect of what is 'acceptable' as a social difficulty is dependent on the social atmosphere of the time. Alcoholism has had many shifts in its perception. It moves between being seen as a disease and as a moral weakness on a fairly regular basis.

In more recent times, the internet and social media has made accessing help and information unbelievably easy. And while putting something on the map does not necessarily create solutions, it can and does create support networks. It has also allowed campaigns to be far more wide reaching and it has given power to many voices to be heard. People I interviewed talked about forums, chat rooms, online diaries and then more recently, Facebook and Twitter as ways of connecting with others and making sense of what was happening to them, or what had happened.

*

For Alison, living with an abusive and violent partner, her challenge was finding a way to keep a diary without it being found by him, and the internet provided the answer.

"When we met, he treated me like I was the best thing on earth but quickly everything changed after we moved in together. One night we came home from the pub and he said, 'You were looking at that bloke, weren't you?' I said I didn't know what he was talking about and his answer was a fist. And from that point on it just degenerated into a really violent relationship. Very quickly I went from being a very happy outward-going girl with a good job, who went to work every day and had lots of friends, to someone who didn't leave the house. I gave up my job because he didn't like that I was out of the house without him - he justified it by saying that he had enough money for us both so I didn't need to work. In reality this was just an excuse to keep me under his control all the time.

I could never even remember what triggered the violence; he was very unpredictable. It could be because I had burnt the dinner, or broken a plate. One time it was because I'd worn a skirt somewhere he'd forbidden it. I remember being dragged out of my parents' house, driven home and dragged down the hall by my hair; he slammed the door against my head over and over. I was constantly bruised, I think I may have had cracked ribs at one point, but he was very clever and it was usually in places it could be hidden.

Somewhere along the way I decided that this was it, this was the way my life was going to be, I might as well accept it. Once he'd broken my spirit the physical violence stopped – he only had to look at me to control me – and we somehow decided to have a family."

At this point a deep sense of shame had overtaken Alison which powerfully informed her that this was somehow her fault and there was no escape. Alison's breakthrough came when she found an online diary and she began to make this unconscious, destructive dialogue conscious through observing herself through the eyes of other people.

"One day I came across an article on websites worth visiting and there was one called Open Diary, it was an online diary. I'd started to write in a journal but was constantly gripped with fear that he might find it, so this online one seemed like a good idea because he didn't really go on the computer much. So I started this diary account and I wrote my first entry and someone left me a note that said 'Welcome to Open Diary, I'm in the UK too, let's be friends.' So initially I started writing about what the kids had been doing – I was child-minding at the time so I would write about my day.

Gradually as time went on I started writing a bit about the relationship and how controlled I felt and why I felt controlled, and then I started talking about the past violence and how things had been, and people responded by saying: 'You've got to get out of there, what are you doing?' It was then that I realised that I wasn't me anymore, I was just a shell of a person going through the motions, I'd lost myself completely because I had buried me away. I couldn't be me, because he didn't like me. I had changed everything: my clothes, my music taste, my opinions. I'd stopped doing the things I enjoyed because he didn't like them. It was easier this way because then there would be no excuse for an argument. I was just a hollow little bit of nothing."

Through her story Alison describes the process of shame. Something was being done to her and not only was she feeling ashamed that it was taking place, but in addition, she was not doing anything about it, and the feeling of powerlessness allowed the shame to spiral into the depths of her internal world. It was only by taking some control through the diary and hearing the reactions of other people (even though they were strangers) that Alison began to make conscious her unconscious world. Telling people about what was happening in her world let the process of healing from shame begin.

"Writing in my diary helped me to realise how wrong my life was and that realisation brought about so much change. Through that diary, I started talking more and more about everything that had happened and how things were now and the more support I got the more I realised that actually *he* was in the wrong, not me. This was the beginning of a long journey to get to where I am now but without that initial connection with others, I'm not sure what would have been the starting point for me."

*

In Chapter 4 Sue talked about the childhood abuse she suffered. The stories of individuals, and research, have shown that shame, self-blame, post-traumatic stress disorder are all characteristic of how someone who experienced abuse as a child may have internalised that experience.

"The long term effects of child sexual abuse can be so pervasive that it's sometimes hard to pinpoint exactly how the abuse affected you. It can permeate everything, your sense of self, intimate relations, sexuality, parenting, work - even your sanity." [8]

Sue has been on this journey of healing, with all of its pains and stops and starts, and learning and growing and eventually she found herself through learning self love. I asked Sue what she would say to other women reading this book who have been through similar things in their lives. What would she want them to read? What would *she*

---

[8] Taken from *The Courage To Heal. A Guide For Women Survivors Of Child Sexual Abuse* by Ellen Bass and Laura Davies. This book was first written in 1988 and has since been published many times and remains a highly recommended book with an opening introduction with the heading of Healing Is Possible.

have wanted to read that would have been helpful? What could a book have said to her that she needed to hear?

"I think in terms of being abused in childhood, you need to understand that it's not you and you're not on your own. I remember not long after it started, I was off school ill at home and I watched a TV programme that happened to be a chat show about child abuse. In those days abuse wasn't widely talked about at all. I remember watching it and this feeling of relief came over me because I thought, 'It's *not* me, it's not my fault and I'm not alone and it happens to other people.' So certainly I'd like to have read that you are not on your own and there is a way out of it; learning to believe in yourself is vital, as is getting help and talking to someone. I didn't do that for many years because I didn't think that I could.

I was ashamed; terribly, terribly ashamed. Even now, as someone who is more willing to talk about it now and open up about it, it's not easy. I still have that deep sense of shame about my childhood, about abuse and about my dad going to prison. These are not things that are very easy to open up about – not exactly dinner table topics!

That sense of shame kept me silent for a long time and that is what kept it all inside me. Once I learned to *trust* friends as I got older and went to university, I did confide in them and that helped me to understand that it wasn't my fault. I think the thing I wish I had realised earlier is that it wasn't my fault, that there was no need for me to have shame. I needed to value myself and love myself. I had spent all of those years drinking on my own at night – it was such a waste; a waste of a tremendous amount of potential. I coped by living in a fantasy world, by having a few drinks, and then I could be everything I didn't feel that I was. To anyone reading this I would say don't waste your life living in a fantasy world, because there is a real life out there to be had and you don't have to move countries like I did, just make small changes that make a difference to how you feel about yourself. There is always a way out, even when you think there isn't – talk to someone. Also, know that you can break a pattern. Just because it happened to you doesn't mean it has to continue; I've shown my son a different life, and I'm very proud of the parent I've become, despite the parenting model I had. I would also say, don't be scared of being the person you want to be."

*

Annett describes her understanding of the road to feeling shame: shame about her body, her femininity and her very existence.

"Love was hard to come by and was often replaced with masses of food, as it was in my case. As a result, I was quite large and I hated myself, but couldn't do anything about it because the subconscious mind control from my parents was at work in my head like an undercover software programme: 'If you don't eat at least a ton of cake and pork in all its possible forms and shapes, you are bad and we won't like you!' Well, perhaps this is slightly exaggerated, but the bottom line is that of course you end up being controlled by this message if you hear it often enough. When you're a teenager and your parents express their disgust about your appearance...presto, the psychological damage is done, for the rest of your life.

Consequently, I didn't do well in school as I was frightened, self-conscious and constantly bullied by my class mates, because I had no social skills to defend myself. After this bad start, I fell into a massive black hole of depression and self-pity. The way with victimhood is that you cannot help yourself and blame everyone else for your bad luck. If a young person gets attacked with messages about how bad and useless they are, it becomes ingrained into their thinking. You eventually accept it as a reality and it reflects to the outer world, which reflects back to you."

Annett lived with a deep shame that affected her entirely. Later she explores how she pulled herself from this pit of shame and despair and internal isolation through the growth and development of her spiritual connection.

*

For Gabby, understanding guilt and shame helped her to move on and forgive herself.

> "I learned that guilt and shame are not the same. Guilt usually goes with thinking 'I did something bad, I made a mistake'; shame is more about 'I am bad and I am a mistake'. I have had to work hard on my own thinking to realise I am worthy of being forgiven, I need to forgive myself, and I need to love myself. "

*

Personal Ramblings

Chapter Nine – Forgiveness Unlocks The Door

"Forgiving is love's toughest work, and love's biggest risk. If you twist it into something it was never meant to be, it can make you a doormat or an insufferable manipulator. Forgiving seems almost unnatural. Our sense of fairness tells us people should pay for the wrong they do. But forgiving is love's power to break nature's rule." - Lewis B. Smedes

In the previous chapter, we looked at shame and making conscious the unconscious, and how this is a kind of starting point, an acknowledgement that things have to change, that we can't go on as we are.

I really understand that while similar themes stand out in each person's recovery, it is not a linear process. There is no single way, a clear approach, a set of steps taken in a certain order, with us moving in one direction until we arrive somewhere that looks like a paradise of painless nirvana. To look at forgiveness really highlights the ongoing nature of healing, self-awareness and the personal responsibility taken when we exercise our choice to change. For me, forgiveness has been something that I have needed to revisit at different times throughout my life, seeking a depth to its meaning, signifying a deepening relationship with myself as time has passed, wisdoms that only time and experience can bring. And because life continues to do what life does, the need to forgive is a recurring theme and the ability to do so eases over time through understanding its power, its benefits and its healing capacity.

In my early experience of recovery, I remember being told or asked, I'm not sure which, "When will you forgive?" The people asking me this were all well-meaning but very much entrenched in their own journey. When confronted with my visual anger they wanted to help me but they didn't give me any of the other bits of information I needed to undergo this impossible looking task and that just made me feel angrier. I actually feel that it just put me in a perpetual cycle of I can't forgive, I'm angry, I feel ashamed, I don't like myself because I can't forgive, I'm angry, I feel ashamed, I don't like myself, and so on.

Maybe if this is an area that you are struggling with, you are stuck in a cycle too. If you can break it and get out, the rewards are abundant. Forgiveness is a really tricky one. It can be used by other people or institutions to silence the anger. It can be used to perpetuate self-loathing because it can seem so elusive and mysterious. It has a religious platform which can also be loaded with childhood issues or control.

Try and see forgiveness in its purest form - as a loving light as opposed to the darkness that can wash over us when we are in pain - and you may be able to make more sense of it.

What can I share with you about forgiveness?

- Forgiving is not about forgetting. I do not believe that there is anything that anyone else has done that is unforgiveable, because forgiveness is not about the other person and what they have done, it is about us. Me. You. This is difficult but it is incredibly important to grasp. When I listen to mothers talking about forgiving their child's murderer, I am humbled. I understand why and how even though I cannot imagine what they went through to be able to get to that point.

- In order to forgive, you have to be willing and you have to be ready. The journey to this point takes as long as it takes.
- I believe that before the process of forgiveness can take place, acknowledging and then coming to a place of acceptance of what has happened and then working through the anger is crucial. Otherwise forgiveness is just another tool to silence the voice of hurt and pain and sense of deep betrayal.
- Forgiveness does not condone what has been done.
- It is an understanding that whatever we do to another to 'punish' them will harm us, not them.
- It is a desire to be free, to move on, and to have an inner peace.

What happens in not forgiving?

- In a state of 'un-forgiveness' I can be a victim. I can be 'done to' by another person, place or thing.
- In this state I can be defined by what has happened to me and I can live it over and over again every day, 'stuck' in my hurt and pain.

- I can recreate the same pain continuously as I attract the situation back into my life because I eat, sleep, breathe what has been done to me.
- I rage, I am bitter, I cannot heal.

For me, forgiveness is a crucial element of my journey. Without it, I am lost. It was this that gave me the freedom of forgiveness and all that it brings. People find their way to forgiveness in many different and ultimately personal ways.

*

"There is no doubt that forgiveness frees us. Forgiveness has the power to heal our bodies, our minds and our spirits – our very lives. But we need to make sure we aren't forgiving just because we think it is the right thing to do or because we are giving in to pressure from others. And we need to make sure that we are not just using forgiveness as another form of denial. True forgiveness occurs only when we allow ourselves to face the truth and to feel and release our emotions, including our anger, about what was done to us." [9]

Following 30 years in corporate senior management Beverley quite literally crashed out in 2009, suffering from ill health. She spent two years on a journey through depression and anxiety before retraining as a life coach in order to help others move their lives forward in a positive way. Here she describes that journey and explains how forgiveness played a huge part in her recovery.

---

[9] Taken from *Healing Your Emotional Self* by Beverly Engel 2006

"For me depression was like a dimmer switch that gradually lowered the light over a period of two years; there wasn't a single sign or moment when I said, 'Oh I have depression'. The true realisation only came to me during a trip to the doctor's in June 2009 when I just couldn't stop crying. As my doctor declared, 'You only have two weeks before you are hospitalised with depression' the truth hit me like a thump in the pit of my stomach. I gasped for air as he made it clear I had to sign off work straight away or I'd be taken to hospital in an ambulance!

The choice was no choice. I walked out of the surgery in a daze. I felt so very alone. The light had quite literally gone off.

From that point on the true effects of that dark journey took their toll. It was difficult even to pull myself out from under the duvet. Family and friends all supported me and helped where they could. The problem was that, over time, they couldn't understand how pulling yourself together wasn't such an easy option.

I came to understand that depression is a form of mental illness which still in some areas holds a stigma and a huge misunderstanding. At its core for me lay stress, anxiety, paranoia, panic attacks and the ultimate - FEAR! Over time all these feelings had become part of my everyday life and boy, was I scared. The positive, happy, successful confident me had been replaced by a negative, shaking, crying mess!

For me, depression changed my life, and through speaking to others with depression I have come to realise that it is as unique to one person as much as that person is unique in themselves.

At times I didn't believe I would survive the dark days of depression. Thoughts of suicide did creep in but they were pushed away by those who stood by me. The strength of my belief in myself somehow always shone a light and when it didn't, others' belief in me certainly did.

Today I enjoy an amazing life, full of love, light and laughter. I have moved back to my home village, I'm in a wonderful relationship and I cherish each moment as a gift. I have surrounded myself with positive living and positive people in the knowledge that it is this that supports the life I now have.

Depression is a very lonely place and as those travelling its journey know, you may well be surrounded by people but in fact whilst this can physically assure you are not alone, it can in turn highlight the loneliness you feel inside.

Forgiveness has been huge for me for so many reasons. It wasn't until I spent time with a counsellor that I realised how much grief I held inside. As I came to forgive so my heart got lighter. How did I forgive? I made a conscious decision to let go of all those who had hurt me because I realised that by carrying them around in my head I was not releasing them from my heart. Repeatedly I would think and say this line from the Bible: 'Forgive them for they know not what they do.' I used it back then and I continue to use it as often as needed.

If somebody told me that my journey with depression would one day turn out to be an experience cleverly disguised as a gift I would never have believed them. However, that is what it has become and it is my hope that through sharing my experience I can light the journey ahead and assure and inspire others to move forward with their lives."

Beverley's recovery from depression was underpinned by forgiveness; such is the powerful nature of this as a tool for healing.

*

Now we have explored the theme of forgiveness of others, we can look at forgiving ourselves. This all fits in with the cycle of shame, hurt, pain, low self-esteem, self-loathing, and how we break it. Whether forgiveness of others or that of self comes first, who can say? I would imagine that it would be a different experience for everyone and as it is likely to be ongoing and an area that is revisited constantly then it may even be unlikely to know what comes first.

Self-forgiveness is the ability to accept our imperfections, to know that mistakes are just learning opportunities, to love ourselves as we are (self-love is the focus in Chapter Eight) and to have respect for ourselves. When we achieve this, this spills over into the world around us. Through judging ourselves less and forgiving ourselves, we will learn to judge others less harshly and forgive them of their humanness. This isn't always easy, especially if you have a very critical edge to your personality, whether you have acquired that through your life experiences or your need for perfection or because you strive constantly to do your very best, no matter how gritted together your teeth are. But forgiving others when we have forgiven ourselves is a natural result, a by-product.

Self-forgiveness is a huge part of living a life and of being 'well'. It is about:

- Taking responsibility for our actions
- Accepting we are flawed, all of us.
- Accepting ourselves, and in doing so stopping the cycle of destructive punishing behaviour
- It forms the basis of us beginning a loving relationship with ourselves as opposed to a punishing, critical, abusive one.

*

Nikki talks about her journey to self-forgiveness in such an eloquent and humbling way, with a very personal take on the prism from which she views the world.

"I've got to a point in my life now where I accept that everybody has a story with a beginning, middle and conclusion. Who knows where I am at this stage, but I have grown to realise that reflections rarely offer the same picture; every time I look, I see something different. To me stories are not real; they are just that, 'stories', so I will present what has happened to me and how I have dealt with it in the hope that my words resonate on some level and others will feel inspired to tell their story in any way they choose and it will reach those it is meant for. My landscape was of a middle class, loving and privileged upbringing, interspersed with conflict, confusion and deep concerns that things didn't feel right, no matter how they looked on the outside.

The first curveball thrown at my parents was the discovery that their five year old daughter had been "inappropriately handled by a builder" who was subsequently caught by the police. Counsellors will always describe their work as helping to peel an onion; I guess this was one of my earlier layers. My teens were simply angry with baggage collected along the way through a broken family, misunderstood adolescent behaviour and a first love who was the victim of my protective barrier. Everything was getting heavy, leading me to seek pastures, countries and continents anew.

The next chapter of my life began on foreign shores and brought me many discoveries and the conflict of immense materialism and poverty that is South East Asia. Life became a similar landscape of what I wanted and what I thought would be a perfect lifestyle and yet something was still missing. I had run away rather than face my demons and was later to repeat our family "divorce" patterns which threw me into a den of self-punishment and complete aloneness. I seemed to be unable to connect deeply with others, however wonderful they were and however much love they gave me. So I had no choice but to stop at the red light and start to understand the connection with myself first. I found a therapist who became one of my earth angels who reflected back to me a wisdom I had forgotten and ignored. For the first time in my life, for one hour a week, I felt totally supported and loved. I cannot say why this unknown lady gave me the space that no one else could offer but I was eternally grateful and she would become the first sign of my ability to 'sense' the future.

My marriage chapter closed and a relationship chapter opened and I was to look into a new mirror. This chapter would be the moment my spirit decided to show its face and I could never ignore it again.

The relationship was brought to a traumatic close one night while I was driving. I had lived my life fully with both mind and body but now my spirit was screaming to be heard. My partner passed away dramatically one November night and from that moment I would no longer live without acknowledging the whole of my being. My mind and body shattered, my spirit would be the voice to lead me to continue my journey with many more corners, traffic lights and curves ahead. Recovering, understanding and soul searching was a particularly long red light. Maybe the lights changed several times without me noticing but I knew that with each orange I would look and when ready I would go on the green light. There was a voice saying 'This is not about blame, this is about learning acceptance, forgiveness, trust.' (The voices were to continue and the road led to a college in London where I trained to use spirit guidance and evidence as a healing tool for other people.)

This period was like being on a flat surfboard, riding the wave. There comes a point when there is no wave; the water simply carries you onto the sand where you stop. This was how I lived. A traumatic event can trigger the shift from a normal three dimensional life to so much more. It's like throwing a stone in the water as the ripples affect everyone. I could not run away or set up any more unhappy situations than the one I had to deal with. I had come to a fork in the road and I took it!

My situation gave me many opportunities to help and become involved in something that had shattered more than a windscreen. A wake up call comes along every now and then which reminds us of the gift of simplicity. When you awaken your soul to help others you start loving yourself enough to believe you can do anything.

Forgiveness was the key to my healing; once I'd mastered forgiveness for myself I knew the rest would follow (and it did). Though on the surface people say a light bulb lights up one day to say enough is enough, we never know what they have been through to get to that point.

The main turning point when I knew life would be changed forever was triggered by the event that ended the life of the man I was in a relationship with, no doubt. For the first time I had to keep my mind and body functional for my children and the trauma meant I slowed to a halt. But from then on people, situations and events simply flowed into my life. I had no control over it, I was simply swimming in the "flow" of existence. At last my spirit (and the spirits of others) had a chance to be heard. My mind was asking how I had got to this point, why had this happened to me and not someone else, and how did I want to move forwards from here in a different way. I came to realise that in the new and developing holistic world I would never engage as a whole person if I left my spirit standing on the sidelines. In times of stillness now (even in a traffic jam) I take an opportunity to enjoy the moment, through listening to great music, people watching, and doing anything else that brings me good feelings.

I continue to read books written by people who have been inspired to share their beliefs and stories and I have found great comfort that it is no longer a 'new age' thing to believe we are all connected. A Buddhist mantra became important to help me detach myself from the belief that all would be OK if I had the right house/partner/possessions. I don't believe I am here to live in poverty but I can help those who do. My learning experience has come about in different ways.

I do believe things happen for a reason, I do believe there is something within destiny and fate that brings us lessons and experiences so we may be able to learn from them and humanise the polarities of love/hate, grief/joy, wealth/poverty - without one you cannot have the other. You really can 'create' a new landscape out of incredibly dark times. When you learn to love and trust yourself others will do the same and it brings the confidence to sow some new seeds of your very own in that garden of your soul. I learnt about forgiveness.

Forgiveness has been the key to finding peace within my garden; it is where I visit in times of stillness, and it is an ever changing landscape but always beautiful; a place where I can check in regularly with myself. I have realised that I am the best I can be at any given time; that knowledge brings a sense of freedom and my spirit smiles every day!

I learnt about acceptance and control. You cannot swim against the flow, no matter how hard you resist. There are powers so much greater than we can imagine and they are willing us to accept our own perfection.

I am grateful every day, I still get angry and I have insecurities and make mistakes (twice if they're fun!), but I have many different viewpoints of my landscape and my story continues...."

Nikki's story is a powerful one, and one that is full of forgiveness for herself and for others.

*

Personal Ramblings

Chapter Ten – Self Love is the Cornerstone to Everything

"Each experience is a stepping-stone in life, including any so-called mistakes.

Love yourself for all your mistakes.

They have been very valuable to you.

They have taught you many things. It is the way you learn.

Be willing to stop punishing yourself for your mistakes.

Love yourself for your willingness to learn and grow."

- Taken from Louise Hay - Heart Thoughts.

Does self-love happen before or after forgiveness? In much the same way as I discussed whether we forgive others or self first in the previous chapter, I would say, who knows? I know not. I do know that without self-love I would have - and be - nothing. Self-love saved me and has been the cornerstone of my recovery and the way I live my life every day. The development of my relationship with myself, and how I view that relationship, is the key to all my other relationships.

Because it's love, one could be excused for thinking this was a fairly straightforward piece of the recovery jigsaw, but self-love takes a lot of work and a re-training of our internal wiring. Within us we have a complex dialogue of voices, acquired through the messages we hear in our childhood, the patterns of behaviour we observe all around us, the models of self-love we see (or don't see), experiences from our education, whether from teachers or peers, successes and 'failures' (That's not a word I like; I prefer "opportunities for learning" but society certainly focuses on failures), from the partners we've chosen and so on.

Even when we have a solid sense of self and a high esteem, sense of value and self-love, things can happen in our lives that knock that right out of our system. It's not all about what happens to us as children but also what happens to us as adults. Childhood is usually a good place to start though, as we take into adulthood patterns of behaviour, good ones and bad. Some things we reject, some things we repeat and then we add our own complex personalities and life experiences to the mix. We are all individuals and there isn't one answer.

Self-Love

When working with clients in my practice, self-love is usually one of the most misunderstood concepts and one of the hardest for people to grasp. It gets confused with self-adoration, arrogance, over-confidence and indulgence.

A useful way to experience self-love is by becoming your own loving parent and treating yourself as you would want a loving parent to treat you, rather than relying on external love from others. Remember, this is not an opportunity for you to start beating yourself up about your own parental behaviour towards your children, nor does it serve as a yardstick by which to think about the way you were parented. This is about you, the adult and your relationship with yourself. Using the concept of a 'loving parent' in relation to self-love gives those of you who don't understand what self-love is some kind of context within which to grasp it. If that doesn't work for you, let it go and think about how you would like to define and makes sense of what self-love means for you.

Another approach is to think in terms of your best friend and what you would do or say to them. Funnily enough, I was on the phone to a friend not long ago, beating myself up about something I should have done, could have done or would have done differently, and quite rightly she just asked me whether I would be so critical of a friend which, of course, I wouldn't. It was a much appreciated little nudge back into my sensible zone, given to me on a plate. You can use the roles of "loving parent" or "best friend" as a yardstick by which you think about how you can treat yourself with kindness, love, warmth and care.

The first time I understood that I had no sense of self-worth or self-love at all was in early recovery from alcoholism. I was in my very early twenties and I believed I was worth nothing. My daily drinking had been replaced with an inordinate amount of coffee that would keep most people awake for a week, enough tobacco to give me the kind of sexy undertone in my voice that men have been known to pay for and three AA meetings a day. Sober I may have been but I was still very much 'using'. At that time, in order to let go of the drink, I needed all these crutches and I am very grateful that I had them for that first year of recovery.

Word on the 'recovery' street was all about Louise Hay and her affirmations and so began my relationship with self-talk, affirmations and a comprehension that I had to re-wire myself. I chose the affirmation "I love myself deeply" but I wanted to vomit every time I said it because in reality I hated myself deeply. Standing in front of the mirror saying "I love myself deeply" as I insisted on making mock vomiting sounds became my amusement for the day. My sheer disgust at saying such a thing was driven by self-loathing and was as much a part of me then as my own skin. Eventually I understood I had two choices: either learn to love myself, or die in the toxic embrace of alcohol, the trusted companion that would one day take me to my premature death. It was then, and only then, that I could say such a thing comfortably, and out loud. Now I can sing it, shout it and write it if need be. I love myself deeply!

So in the context that I've given, what would a loving parent do? They would:

- Provide regular nutritional food
- Ensure regular sleep patterns
- Be kind and gentle and unconditional in their communications
- Express love and affection
- Offer praise
- Be consistent
- Avoid criticism
- Listen to your needs
- Help you feel safe
- Encourage responsibility

Hopefully that gives you some understanding of self-love and how the lack of these things creates an environment of negative relationships, poor choices, low self-esteem and self-destructive behaviour patterns.

*

Alex, who helped me with the transcripts for this book, describes her journey to understanding self-love and uses the parenting concept as well. Her journey was brought about through the life changing experience of having Chronic Fatigue Syndrome.

> "Developing self-love was a huge turning point for me in regaining at least my emotional health. I had a mother who didn't love herself and as a consequence I never learned to love myself either. I now believe it to be one of the most important pieces of everyone's wellness jigsaw.
>
> I needed to hit rock bottom to work it out - I needed for my so-called nearest and dearest to turn their backs on me and kick me whilst I was down and to feel utterly alone and crushed before I realised that I didn't need love from other people, I could love myself - it was a light bulb moment.
>
> I separate the word 'myself' into *my self*, and that makes me understand it more. I bring to mind a picture of myself which I love, from when I was about 8 years old and completely lovely and happy, but vulnerable - this is who I think of when I think of my self. I treat my self like I would treat that little girl; I am her protector and best friend. When I first started to think about myself this way, I realised

how badly and unfairly I had treated myself all these years and I promised never to let that happen again.

This has helped me to cultivate more self-respect and be courageous enough to say no, when I need to (something I was too afraid to do before). It also means that I feel stronger and more grounded. I have more confidence now as well."

The process of self-love is so succinctly put by Alex, even down to her picturing herself as a child, happy and free and knowing that that child is still a part of the adult.

*

After her recovery from breast cancer Kelly didn't recognise herself, to the point where she couldn't even look at herself in the mirror. Life had thrown feelings of self-loathing at her.

"In order to move beyond my breast cancer I had to accept the new me... the post cancer Kelly. I didn't know who I was anymore. I didn't recognise the unfamiliar image in the mirror, with my post chemo hair (or should I say lack of), my scars and my new body shape after my mastectomy. Not only did I not recognise the girl staring back at me in the mirror, I didn't know what she was about. What did she want out of life? What was important to her? What were her dreams and desires?

Unfortunately for me, the new Kelly wasn't new in the way that is fresh and exciting, immaculate and with a guarantee. As far as I was concerned this was more faulty goods, flawed and damaged.

Enter Gok Wan and his team. They helped me to develop a new relationship with my body and gradually, little by little, I accepted the body I found myself in. I realised that no one keeps the body they have when they are young. We all age, or shall we say gain character! Sure, my scars weren't quite the laughter lines I might have hoped for, but nevertheless they were part of the person I had become.

They say time is a great healer, and that is true. Little by little, I got to know the Kelly I had become. I learned to accept my scars. I replaced the repulsion I felt when I looked in the mirror with pride and a sense of accomplishment of how I had coped and how far I had come. I got to know who I was and what I wanted out of life. I learned to love myself again. I found new confidence in ME! Only then could I move on. Only then could I dream new dreams."

*

Sue's long and difficult recovery from endless and plentiful childhood abuse embedded within her a deep self-loathing that left unimaginable emotional scars.

"For years I harboured a core belief about myself that I was not good enough. Unwittingly my job as a teacher reinforced that. I taught for 18 years, and for the last ten of them, easily, I was desperate to get out. Friends and family thought I had some sort of strange complex about being a teacher, and any kind of perceived criticism would make me see red, often have me in tears. There have even been friends I have not spoken to for years because of my reaction.

It's only now that I have lost that core belief, and now know that I am more than good enough, that I realise what was going on. For every report that said 'Teachers are useless, letting down the country, ruining children's lives' and so on, I substituted 'Sue' for 'teacher'. That lack of self-love led to years of misery and daily loathing about who I was and what I did, and in hindsight I realise it was myself I couldn't stand, not the job. I must have spent a good ten years being ashamed of what I did for a living, on top of being ashamed of my childhood! Learning to love myself has been the single biggest step I think I have taken, and it has had the most profound effect."

*

This is key and this really needs to be understood alongside some sort of understanding of what self-love actually is. Self-love can come from absolutely nowhere else than from yourself. No partner, no job, no drug, no amount of travelling, no children, no drink, no food, no car, no bank balance will give you self-love. Contrary to just about everything that you may have thought you understood about gratification and reward, none of it means anything at all.

Until you love who you are, you forgive yourself, you accept yourself just as you are, with all your flaws and lovely bits, only then can the process of loving yourself begin. Once you are on this road, you will need to work on loving yourself on a daily basis until it becomes closer to second nature than not.

"Success is liking yourself, liking what you do, and liking how you do it." - Maya Angelou

Annett recalls her journey to self-love.

> "In my mid-twenties I had enough of all of it. I sought refuge and retreated for a couple of months into a farm that stood empty, trying to find answers to what was happening to me and how to help myself. A few books were given to me, like The Celestine Prophecy which explained perfectly how we all manipulate each other in order to get energy, which in turn makes us feel good, so we start creating role plays in order to get more of that same energy. This was probably the first time I came into contact with anything esoteric or metaphysical and I didn't exactly know what to do with it then. But today, it makes complete sense to me when I look back at how my life has unfolded. All the pieces of the puzzle have been laid out along the way, so that I didn't forget why I came here and what my job was...namely to learn to give what I

didn't receive - i.e. love, and especially self-love! - and to keep that love alive in the midst of the worst drama."

When you have a loving relationship with yourself, you'll find that your relationships with other people, places and things change too. From this we start to grow. Previous negative behaviours have nowhere to fester and negative relationships that have felt comfortable or serviced our self-loathing will fall away, sometimes dramatically or sometimes with ease.

Forgiveness, gratitude, releasing of shame, acceptance; these are all the ingredients you need to create a loving relationship with yourself.

*

Personal Ramblings

Chapter Eleven – Connecting to our Spiritual Self

I cannot imagine a life without being on a spiritual path and yet there was definitely a time when I couldn't have imagined me even saying that. Born in 1970 in a home run by nuns for unmarried mothers, I went on to spend the following ten years being brought up in a house with my mother and my gran, a French Catholic from the Victorian era, a survivor of two world wars. One day, after watching the film *Ben Hur*, I remember her saying to me somewhat aggressively in her thick French accent, "You see Leeza, now you must believe in God." Hollywood had spoken! My lovely grandmother was very much of her generation and very much a believer in her religion without any exploration of it. She just had a plain old acceptance of the order of things and I could not bear it. I found religion to be dogmatic, punishing and hypocritical, abhorrent with its unquestioning of anything. I absolutely could not connect with any of it.

I rejected it with force and only considered the spiritual aspect of myself again when I went to AA and the concept of a Higher Power was presented to my broken, twenty year old self. I was told in no uncertain terms that I was not the centre of the universe and I needed to find something to hand over my will and my life to. When things got painful, I was to speak to my Higher Power. For all anyone cared it could be the sea, or a double decker bus - but I needed one! So I got one; my higher Power was to be the sea and the seeds were sown for me to develop my connection with my spiritual self and for me to recognise my needs in this area. Like my emotional, physical and mental self, my spiritual self needed nurturing and tending to as well.

This thread of acceptance that our spiritual paths need nurturing is one of the themes that run through the lives of people enjoying a life of wellness after adversity. So what does this actually mean? For me I believe it means:

- To seek wisdom
- To strive for personal growth
- To exercise a tolerance and forgiveness of others
- To seek a deeper connection with others
- To give to others generously
- To work towards a sense of complete trust that 'everything will be ok'

We all have our own definitions and understanding of our spiritual path (which, incidentally, is a path we choose to walk on every day, rather than a destination to which we are trying to get), whether that is through an organised religion or not. It matters not. The main thing is To Thine Own Self Be True, a fundamental underpinning to your own journey.

Annett learnt to understand the journey to her spiritual path through all that has happened to her.

> "Discovering that I had a natural talent for art was quite a shock for me because I had always been rejected by everyone throughout my life and I thought I was stupid, worthless and a total waste of space. So that moment was the first time that I felt

some sort of success in my life, and my time at university literally helped me to break through my severe depression. Suddenly I had all these wonderful creative people around me who were really open minded and loving. It was like suddenly someone had poured nourishing water over my head and I started to blossom. I loved it so much and soon realised that this was it! This was what I wanted to do with my life. Live the free, bohemian life of an artist.

All it needed was the influence of a proper role model that came in form of a highly sensitive soul. People stepped into my life and triggered a need for me to work on myself. They really were so open hearted and just affected everyone with their presence. So naturally, I wanted to be close to them all the time, but I had to realise that they didn't want me to cling onto them and suck their energy. I had to find it first in my own heart, then bring it out and nourish it before someone else could love me.

I am now a professional artist and educator with my own company, Indigo Visions. I facilitate workshops, write articles and also co-manage a spectacular art gallery in Ramsgate, Kent, which is a true project of passionate self-realisation and proof that dreams do indeed come true. It is called The Monkey Cage Gallery and has been given to me by God like a trophy in exchange for all my hard work and persistence over the years. I am blessed beyond belief to be able to work in this amazing space that combines highly progressive ideas with beautiful contemporary art and spirituality. I am now in a position where I need to apply everything that I have learned over the years and I love it so much. I couldn't possible do anything more enjoyable. It suits me perfectly and I am totally thriving in this role!

I am also the author of the blog '2012 Ascension Help' and I spent the last six years studying the history of the universe and the nature of our reality, trying to find out why we are all here and indeed what is going to happen to us. An amazing jump in consciousness is occurring and we are all part of it! We will remember that we are all spirit in human form; that we design our lives the way we want them and we put all these obstacles there in order to experience the worst and very best possible things. Karma is coming to an end now and we have to balance Polarity, meaning finishing this Duality Integration Game and moving into Oneness. So these are really cutting edge concepts I concern myself with. What an amazing transformation from where I started out, don't you think?

I came to the conclusion that everything is in our lives because we have invited it. Additionally, any kind of human suffering or personal trauma can only happen because we are not following our life path. Think about it: it's quite a misconception that people think 'Oh, we have this great life, flashy technology and look how comfortable we are!' But in fact we live in the darkest of ages and suffer terribly on an emotional and a spiritual level. This is the truth and the essence of all the spiritual teachings: we in the western world don't love and respect ourselves enough! You *need* to very clearly ask yourself what makes you most happy, what makes you feel light, connected and alive. What do you desire that will bring love and peace to yourself and the planet, that will fully occupy your whole being? Once you have defined these goals, don't compromise for anything less. Give your worries to your angels, ask for help and they will take care of it. Guaranteed! I have often said:

> *"It is my intention that I experience a harmonious lifestyle.*
> *It is my intention that I experience health and energy that lead me to creative adventures.*
> *It is my intention that I am well provided for, that shelter and food and all of the things I need for life will be given to me in great abundance.*
> *I will then pass this great abundance on and share it with others."*

Visualisation definitely works. Through the positive words *'I am a beautiful, intelligent, slim, youthful and successful woman who inspires others!'* I managed to bring that into my reality. You just need to sincerely ask for it, believe in it and you will receive it. Be grateful for everything you've got and trust that it will all work out. That's how you do it. Pray and you'll see that new, beautiful things will happen every day. So you can just sit back, relax and watch your life improve.

People must empower themselves first and increase their frequency in order to function properly. Don't blame your past, your family, or your upbringing. Forgive everyone and let go. It's fair enough to acknowledge your journey and to look back and say: 'OK, I had a bad start, but now I see that it was necessary to learn from it and to come out of it.' It's definitely most important to develop self-love, self-respect and to take responsibility for one's actions. If you are not in tune with your heart, everything in your life will fall apart. Make space for new things to come to you and allow yourself to receive all the abundance in the universe. Take risks, go forward and ask to be placed in a situation where you are best of service to the world."

*

A bout of ante-natal and post natal depression, coupled with the end of Julie's marriage to her childhood sweetheart and the loss of his extended family, led her on a spiral of depression, poor self-esteem and a search for an understanding as to what had happened to her. She found Reiki and started on the journey of recovery.

Reiki has been mentioned a few times and has underpinned the recovery of a few of the contributors. For those of you that may be unfamiliar with it, Reiki is the transfer or channelling of the Universal Life Force Energy, the infinite energy of the Universe that is transferred from one person to another through something called attunement.

The hands are placed on the body through clothes or not, it doesn't matter, and the body's own energy field is rebalanced, allowing the body to feel deeply relaxed through this process of gaining harmony within. The sensation is one of deep relaxation and a feeling of centeredness. It is very soothing and very comforting and can form the basis of the healing process. It is also completely embedded in pure unconditional love and compassion which in itself paves the way for a deep sense of wellbeing and connectedness.

> "It was Reiki that gave me the strength and the self-confidence to pick myself up and carry on. If it wasn't for that I would have stayed within my four walls. The Reiki practitioner actually said to me: 'Your future is not going to come knocking at your front door, you've got to get yourself out there and create your own future,' and it was only with the strength of Reiki that I did manage to do that. I also experimented with affirmations at the time. One of the very first affirmations I used when I was going

through the divorce court was 'Whatever happens, I know I can handle it, I am a very capable person'. And repeating that also gave me the confidence to think 'I can do this'.

I still have these affirmations on display where I can clearly see them and I use them whenever I need them. This journey started when the children were very little and I was alone every evening, which sometimes felt very isolating. I wasn't lonely very often, but I learned that the one person I am with forever is me; I am my own best friend. I had to love myself so I could be loved again.

I developed a level of trust in the Universe that everything happens for a reason, in the perfect time/space sequence, so what is meant to happen will happen at the right time and my journey is very much about letting go of control. In doing this, life will flow more easily. I have learnt that the more I try and control things, the more resistance I'm putting up and I will end up blocking things."

Julie's spiritual path focuses on the Universe as her guide. Whatever we use - Jesus, Allah, Gandhi, The Universe or The Sea (!) - really doesn't matter. I have read many different spiritual and religious teachings and the general themes all seem to me to be remarkably similar.

"I came to realise that I've lived most of my life in my head, completely in my head; being a routine person, getting on with daily life without stopping to notice or ask myself how I actually feel about something or whether I want to be doing something.

For me, spirituality, embracing difference, gratitude, self-love and self-esteem really resonate with how I pulled myself out of that time in my life. Self-love and building my self-esteem is an ongoing process that is now a part of my everyday conscious living, and I feel this is one of the major lessons from the whole experience, along with forgiveness. Like everyone I experience good days and bad days, but I know that I have to learn to love myself before anything else. I now bring gratitude into my daily life for the things that I have rather than the things that I *don't* have."

*

Chrissie left the self help books to one side when she was looking for guidance and inspiration.

"The ones I looked at were almost more spiritual because of another thing that happened in my life: my father died, which made me realise that I did need some beliefs, and they've developed in a spiritual capacity. I was raised a Catholic which was all the guilt thing and the God thing and the church and I really didn't like the religion at all, so I moved away from it. So for me, being spiritual means believing that our lives aren't accidental, that we've chosen these lives and it's up to us to make the best of them. We are all capable of that, we just need to believe that we can do it.

The books I read have tended to be more along the lines of the Law of Attraction and the fact that if you really *really* believe that you can do something, you *can* do it. It's come to fruition so many times in my life and I find that unbelievable. Sometimes when I read the explanation behind it, it does sound a bit like science fiction, but hey, it works! If you've got a passion and those beliefs, then you can make it happen and I think people think that it's only the Richard Bransons and Mother Theresas of this world that can do that, but it's not. There are lots of normal people who are doing very good things out there, within the scope of their lives.

You don't have to self-flagellate yourself to touch people's lives, or to fulfil your own purpose. And I think that's what perhaps puts people off at times, they think they are not capable of it and yet everybody is."

When I interviewed Chrissie, I loved her phrase "in the scope of their lives" because that underpins my message, which is that we all have the capacity to change and grow and recover but it may well have to be within the scope of what we have available to us - and that's ok! Mountains come in all shapes and sizes.

*

Whatever path we choose, we are saying that we need more than what we thought we could create for ourselves alone. Ultimately, we are in a place of love when we do this - love of ourselves and of each other and of all humanity.

"Surrender to God means surrender to love.....The mind's function is to experience love....Once we get to the point where we realise that God is love, it's not too difficult to understand that following God just means following the dictates of love. The hurdle we have to face next is the question whether or not love is such a wise thing to follow. The question is no longer "What is God?" The question we ask now is "What is love?" Love is energy." [10]

I cannot find a better explanation than this one from Marianne Williamson. If you were ever in any doubt as to how to think of connecting with a Higher Power in order to begin to live a more spiritually connected life, then I think understanding that you are surrendering to love has to be the simplest and most accessible place to start.

*

---

[10] This is taken from A Return to Love by Marianne Williamson, p18-19

Personal Ramblings

Chapter Twelve – Giving for the sake of giving

"I have found that among its other benefits, giving liberates the soul of the giver." - Maya Angelou

"It is literally true that you can succeed best and quickest by helping others to succeed." -Napoleon Hill

Taking an experience or a variety of experiences and then doing something positive with them to help other people was a theme that I knew would run through everyone's story. The idea of 'giving back' is not new, of course. It's a fundamental aspect of most spiritual and religious teachings and of many great leaders. Many have literally given their lives for a cause they have believed in for the betterment of humanity; think Martin Luther King, Mahatma Gandhi, Malcolm X, Emily Pankhurst ...

When Chrissie embarked upon Single With Kids, I'm not sure she had any idea how powerful an organisation it would become. Not only did she create budget holidays for low income families, but she created a forum that has become a national support network for single parents. Chrissie works tirelessly on the forum, providing masses of advice, creating stimulating discussions, connecting people who have similar experiences and being an advocate for single parents through providing a voice to the media. All of this came through her own experience of being a single parent – some giving back then might be done without even realising it.

> "It's strange because when we started Single With Kids, it was never the aim of it being a holiday

organisation, it was basically a resource, a support network for single parents and it's really almost guided its own path. The idea obviously was that single parents don't have any network and are often excluded from traditional married set-ups and you do feel ostracised, but the thing that has really motivated me is that my career was very commercial and I would do great things to brands and would add millions to turnover, yet the first testimonial we had from Single With Kids said that we had changed someone's life. That just overshadowed everything else because you are dealing with something that people will remember, especially the children. When you see some of the children talk about their favourite Single With Kids trips on Facebook it's nice to know that we are actually doing something that is enhancing somebody's *life,* you know, it's not giving them a new kitchen appliance or a few figures in a bank account, it is actually something that in many cases is helping them get back on track and helping them turn their lives around. When we read the testimonials we get, we sit there with tears in our eyes, because some of them are extremely moving.

There are thousands of families we've had contact with now because of all the camping trips we organise. There are other holiday organisations out there, of course, but they don't cater for the same families we cater to. They're fine if you've got £2000 to spend, but if you are pushing to spend

£20 on a holiday, you're left behind - and quite often it's those very people who do need the break. Single parent families have the same challenges as every other family and then some, because they're often challenged financially too, and yet there was nobody there to actually give them a break or give them a helping hand.

We also created the forum, which has become a provider of mutual support and I think that's been the important thing. It's great for us now to see people who joined us in the early days who were absolutely in *despair* and at the end of their tether, to see them actually giving back to others on the forum because they've been through it all. Everyone does have a very similar path one way or another; they might have had similar stop off points, you know, but from A to B there are some very significant steps and it's quite interesting to see those people now that they are out of the mire, actually helping others and it's working really well. It's that sharing of experience, of giving something back that helps your own self esteem as well which in itself will help those people to move forward and kick start their lives again."

*

Sarah explains how it wasn't so much about consciously giving but that in dealing with the situation in front of her she gained so much and learnt an important lesson about not always being able to be the centre of your world.

"It's true that if you are full of misery and self-hatred you aren't able to offer much to those around you. However, achieving happiness is not always about doing what you want to do or doing what's right for yourself.

If I'd done what was right for 'me' over the last 3 years I'd be a million miles from where I am now, geographically and emotionally. I'd probably be on a beach somewhere exotic and remote running a lovely little organic café. I'd be a very selfish person and I very much doubt I'd sleep particularly well either.

What I've done is learned to cut my emotional cloth to suit my circumstances. I haven't undervalued myself in doing this; I have simply re-balanced my values. I have moved away from 'self' to 'selves' to incorporate my new responsibilities. Doing this has helped me learn to embrace those responsibilities instead of resent them.

Other outcomes of this is that my family is much closer, achieved partly by my actions but we achieved it together, without any doubt. Our relationships are stronger - after all, they have been stress tested pretty exhaustively. And I have matured emotionally, and the payback for doing so is so much greater than pleasing myself at the cost of all else."

*

Kelly explores perfectly how giving is not necessarily altruistic by definition.

> "I don't believe there is such a thing as giving for the sake of giving. I don't give in the hope that I will receive something from the receiver, but from what I will get back from myself. I give because of how it makes me feel.
>
> In my case, I give my time and my story. I share my story by speaking at events, conferences and support groups, in the hope and belief that it helps others. Each time I tell the story of where I have been and how I have got to where I am today, I give a little bit of myself. I am now in a good place, but when I talk about the personal feelings I had in my darkest days I am instantly transported back to a place I never want to revisit. It is a painful place to be.
>
> So why do I do it? I do it because my hope and belief that my story helps others has been replaced with the knowledge that it does just that. I get amazing feedback and that, put simply, makes me feel good. It makes me feel better about myself. And even on days when I am not feeling so bright, the knowledge that someone else might just be having a better day because of the words and insights I have shared with them makes me feel better.
>
> The process of giving in this way helps me to believe in myself. It is not a selfless act, far from it. I

give because of the joy of seeing how it makes others feel. You see, joy is circular and interactive. I smile, you smile. I laugh, you laugh. They say a smile is the only contagious thing we should share. But I disagree. Joy, laughter and hope can all be passed on.

I went to a Catholic primary school and although I do not hold those religious beliefs now I am truly grateful for some of the lessons that were taught in this religious context. One of those was to treat others how we would hope to be treated ourselves.

I have received great love and support during difficult times in my life, often from the most unexpected people. Somehow it brings even more joy to receive words and acts of kindness from those we don't know well or even at all, doesn't it? I hope too that if and when I need such support in the future, it will be there for me. I don't believe that we deserve to receive such kindness if we don't also give what we expect to receive. Maybe I am banking my good deeds in an account ready for emptying in the future, but I hope that is not the case. Rather, I hope to leave an inheritance of kind words and support that I have been able to share not only with those I know and care about personally but also with those I have not yet met. Whether any of us have the strength to give more than we receive is something that we test during our lifetimes. There are certainly those that do and they give us all something to aspire to."

*

There are so many things we can give; our time, love, care, gifts, experience, wisdom, knowledge, compassion, warmth, money, shelter, food. It matters not that the giver benefits as much as the receiver; there are no negatives in this situation. But it is generally accepted that giving forms a healthy basis for spiritual connection, enhanced relationships with self and others and raised self-esteem as a direct benefit. It's what's known as a win win situation.

*

Personal Ramblings

Chapter Thirteen – Gratitude

"If you want to turn your life around, try thankfulness. It will change your life mightily."- Gerald Good

Gratitude, a feeling of thankfulness and appreciation, has the power to transform each moment and each experience in the most unassuming way. The first time I heard anyone talk about gratitude, I was in my early twenties and I was told that writing about gratitude would help me in my really dark moments. Some days all I could write was "Today I am grateful for the food I have eaten." Other days I could run ten things off my list. But something magical happens in that moment when you focus on what you *do* have; what you *don't* have becomes irrelevant. Your abundance becomes glaringly obvious as you realise that even in times of hardship you may well be able to say "I have my health" (anyone without it knows how amazing a statement that is) or "I have food" (anyone feeling the pangs of hunger through not having enough food would love to say that) or "I have the most beautiful friend(s)", and so on.

Gratitude sits firmly and comfortably on the sofa with your spiritual connection and positive framing and resilience. The way we view the world and how we are within it is extremely powerful for personal change and growth. Expressing gratitude frees you from suffering. Simple.

Beverley explores what it means for her.

> "Following my journey through depression I truly discovered what being 'thankful' was all about.

Never before had I realised how many people I had in my world that really cared. This in itself taught me not to take anything for granted but to be grateful for all the little things as well as the huge big things that come into your life. I was so grateful at that time for the family and friends I had in my life; I had nothing to give them but it never stopped any of them giving me the most important thing they could - time! It was the greatest gift they spared and today I am so grateful for every minute each and every one of them gave.

When I was first asked to write a gratitude list very near the top I had all my senses; I have a very good friend who is visually impaired and he taught me that things many of us take for granted should be treated with respect and gratitude on a daily basis. Nic is an amazing man who travels the world, goes to the cinema (that was a crazy fun evening!!), plays the keyboards and sings on cruise ships; the gentlest soul with a huge heart who explains his lack of sight as 'I am blind, not disabled'. To those of us who have our sight it would seem a nightmare but to Nic it just a part of life; he has never had sight but boy, can he see! He sees things that others miss, he sees a gentle lending hand that guides the way, he sees an open heart when one is there to help, he sees the truth in people therefore he knows who to trust and he sees the positives in so many situations.

It is through lessons like these that I learnt so much about gratitude for it is not the tangible things that we have, the physical nor the perceived beauty, it is the unseen that holds the truest of gifts and it is that for which we should all be truly grateful every day."

*

Kelly talks us through the loss of health, the grief that followed that loss and how gratitude helped her turn around her suffering into something that essentially became positive.

"When things aren't going our way it is easy to focus on what we have lost. For me that was my health, and along with that went my dreams and the future I had planned. I went through a process of grief. Grieving for what you have lost is an important process. At the other side of that process I found acceptance. It is hard to be grateful for anything during grief. You are, by the very nature of the process, concentrating on what you have lost. In a sense you are looking back at what you had. Acceptance only comes when you move from the past into the here and now. Being thankful for what you have rather than what you have lost means that you are focusing on the present. So for me gratitude was a stop I had to pass through on my journey from loss to acceptance, from the past to the present, and ultimately to a future.

This of course is all very easy to say. It is not so easy to be grateful for what you have when you feel like everything you have hoped and worked for has been taken from you. I am not saying 'look on the bright side' in a flippant way. If one more person says to me 'There is always someone worse off,' well, I won't be responsible for my actions. What I am saying is that it is easy to lose focus on all the good things in your life when there is so much pain. Somehow despair, fear and sadness push aside the positive emotions that you have. But by refocusing on the present and being grateful for what you do have the scales can tilt, and somehow you can find room for hope, optimism and joy.

Cancer took many things from me: my health, my hair, my breast, but it gave me so much too. I have met some wonderful people that I would never have met if it had not been for my illness, including Gok! I have had some wonderful experiences, and in a funny way I have gained time - time with my friends and family; quality time that I would not have had if I had been working 9 to 5 for the past five years. So rather than concentrate on what I have lost, I choose to focus on what I have gained. Gratitude is a powerful emotion which for me has brought positivity. And it is an emotion we have control over. We can choose to be thankful and to focus on the positives, and therefore take control of our lives at times when we may feel all control has been lost.

During the filming of my revisit programme for How to Look Good Naked I met up with Gok again and I explained that I had accepted my cancer and if I could I wouldn't change it. I got some criticism for that on one of the breast cancer internet forums. I guess the women that made those comments were in a different place. They questioned how I could say that when breast cancer had brought them and their families so much pain.

I was coming at it from a different angle. Of course I would never have chosen cancer as part of my life. But I had reached acceptance and was coming at it from a position of gratitude. I was focusing on the positives and the things I had gained. And I mean it, I wouldn't want to turn the clock back and miss out on all the wonderful experiences I have had, and the relationships I have made, as a result of my illness. If I could have spared myself and my family the pain and suffering that has been brought to us by cancer then of course I would. But the reality is I can't. I can't change what has happened, but I can change my attitude; and as they say, 'gratitude is the best attitude'."

*

"Be thankful for what you have; you'll end up having more. If you concentrate on what you don't have, you will never, ever have enough." - Oprah Winfrey

*

Ann talks about how she used gratitude to better understand being made redundant and all the good things that came out of it.

> "Things happen for a reason. I am grateful that I was made redundant so that I could be there to bring my daughter through her illness. If I had still been working, I don't believe she would have recovered as well; she needed complete rest for three months and it meant that I did not have to rely on others to look after her. Being made redundant also allowed me to re-evaluate the direction my life was taking and again without the redundancy I would not be at university doing something I love. I am thankful for all the love and support received from my friends during this time.
>
> I'm so thankful to an online community that I found that introduced me to some wonderful friends who I moan to, enjoy great times with and listen to; these are now lifelong friends. Life is brilliant with all those guys about."

*

"Acknowledging the good that you already have in your life is the foundation for all abundance." -Eckhart Tolle

*

Ultimately, gratitude is where your focus shifts from what you perceive you 'lack' to what you actually have. Practising gratitude every day as your default position will help you develop resilience, strengthen your relationships and reduce stress levels. It is by appreciating what you have in life that you become unable to see all that you don't have. And one of the major consequences is that you attract into your life people who are also grateful. When the thoughts and constant chatter within you change from self-pitying negativity to grateful positivity you start to give out different messages which then attract different people; people who can add something to your life rather than wanting to take something away. If this is a big behaviour shift for you then this is where 'fake it to make it' comes into its own. You can start doing this at any time; just develop an awareness of your inner dialogue, turn it around until it becomes your natural state and see and feel the difference.

You can take this as far as you like outside your own thinking. I personally watch very little TV, am very specific about which newspaper articles I read, choose who I spend my time with very carefully and am dedicated to the removal of negativity from any social media sites I am on. In other words, I choose to be around people that embrace life, take personal responsibility and seek to give rather than to get. I take this aspect of my recovery very seriously but we are all different and bringing gratitude into your own inner thinking is the best place to start! It is within this shift that an appreciation of ourselves can be found. If you think negatively about others and about your life then you can be certain that you think negatively about yourself.

Gratitude, self-love and giving back are all intrinsically linked to each other, which is why they are part of a daily shift in 'being' rather than something you do and it's done; it's a way of life, of being, of seeing and of doing.

*

Personal Ramblings

Chapter Fourteen – Resilience and positive framing

"The tragedy of life is not that it ends so soon, but that we wait so long to begin it." – W. M. Lewis

The ability to deal with life and what it sends us is where we need resilience. Dealing with everything from the everyday pressures right through to life changing traumas and still being able to manage and function and, later, to reflect, learn and grow, are all characteristic of being resilient. There are things in life that we have no control over but how we approach them is where the key lies to what we gain from them. The question is whether we all have the capability of resilience and to what extent our differing levels of it affect how we deal with life.

Resilience doesn't stop life from doing what life does, but people who have it are far more able to deal with pressure, disappointment, loss, adversity and unexpected change. It allows people not only to survive something but sometimes to go on and thrive and then actually prosper from it.

- It is believed that resilience is not the trait of a few, but that within most of us is the ability to have it. In other words it is a skill, which is good news because skills can be learnt. It is possessed by ordinary people, not extraordinary people.
- It seems to me that there are some common themes around being resilient. Some good

starting points in developing resilience would be to:

- Remove negative language from your inner dialogue. Telling yourself that you are a failure/not good enough/unlikeable etc will not move you forward. Negative language keeps you stuck. By focusing on your strengths you will build your confidence and self esteem.
- Find a purpose. Charities are more often than not borne out of an experience.
- Nurture yourself. Take care of your health and wellbeing through eating well, sleeping well, exercising, spending time with people you love and who love you. Go for a walk and enjoy that time as reflection time, helping you to clear your head and gain any perspective you may need.
- Learn to accept yourself exactly as you are - imperfections and all.
- Develop a support network with people who do things that you like to do too. Get involved with your community and build your relationships with a wide range of people.
- Learn to live in the day, and then in the moment in that day. Pain and an overwhelming sense of 'I just can't manage this' can feel more manageable when it only has to be dealt with for a 24 hour period. Another similar take on this is to think about how whatever you're feeling will feel in 6 hours from now. 6 days, 6

weeks, 6 months, 6 years? This helps you understand what is really important and what is likely to not overwhelm.

- Positive thinking is powerful. Never underestimate the power your own thoughts have on how you deal with a situation. That's why affirmations and reframing your language are such well used tools. Tell yourself where you want to be, how you want it to look, over and over again; this is an affirmation. Why me? becomes Why not me? This changes your negative language into positive language. For example, I believe that all of what has happened to me was so I could write this book for you. How can that not make perfect sense?!

- Do something outside your comfort zone. This gives you the experience you need to understand that you are capable of something you might not have thought you could do. Jumping out of a plane for a charity might be a bit drastic but it definitely takes you out of your comfort zone (unless you're an adrenalin junkie, which I'm personally absolutely not).

- Many of the themes that run through this book are based around resilience, so use each chapter as you need it to further your understanding and development of a particular area.

Kelly shares her understanding of resilience and how she 'faked it to make it' and learnt that in doing so she retained her power at a time when she felt utterly powerless.

"For me, to be resilient means to be hardy, irrepressible, quick to recover, strong, and tough. Can any of us really be strong and tough in all situations? Or do we simply portray strength on the outside while we cower on the inside? And what if our strength is purely a facade? I believe our outer strength can translate into inner strength. Well, that was my experience anyway. When people asked me how I was doing, I often gave them a positive outlook. And the response gave me the energy and support that I needed to believe my positive words. 'You are doing so well,' 'Your positivity is inspiring,' 'Look how far you have come,' etc etc. I needed to hear those words. They gave me the strength that I had led others to believe I already had.

We don't have to be tough all the time. There is also strength in showing our weaknesses and being honest about our feelings when things are difficult. I think the key is to think carefully about who you confide in and in what circumstances.

No one wants to go to dinner on a Friday night and be sat next to 'Mrs Gloom and Doom'. In those situations I never responded to the question 'How are you doing?' with a negative answer. I saved my crying and my shaking for intimate moments with close friends and family. As a result I carried on being invited to social events. I was able to contribute to life outside my own little cancer bubble, even if my contribution was substantially reduced by my physical condition. I didn't want to be treated like a patient. I didn't want others taking away my control by making decisions for me. 'Oh we won't invite her to watch the movie with us on Saturday. I don't think she is up to it,' that kind of thing. By being positive on the outside I took self-control. I gave others the permission to give me the power back to make my own decisions, and I took strength from that.

You are what you believe. If you think you can't cope then you probably won't. If you believe that you can find joy in life when all about you is crumbling, then that joy will come to you.

None of us can be positive all the time. Often strength can be found in believing that life will get better. Life is like a bicycle. To maintain balance we have to keep moving. We have to look beyond the rough terrain, the obstacles we need to get over, the pitfalls we might fall into; we have to look to the horizon, where the sun shines."

I love Kelly's understanding of strength within vulnerability but also knowing that there are places where we are safer than others to express our innermost turmoil. I believe that it is very much a mistake to confuse vulnerability as a sign of weakness. I would also say that about openness and kindness. All these things require strength of the heart and the spirit.

*

Gabby also recognises that she used her inner strength to 'fight' her way through cancer but in doing that, she could regain some of her power in a situation that must have left her feeling powerless.

> "The people who survive plane crashes are not the ones who sit meekly awaiting instructions from the flight crew. The ones who always survive have a compelling reason why they must live - usually the people they love. With this love surging through them, they will fight their way off the plane, demanding to be saved.
>
> This was my attitude to my cancer treatment. My medical team were great, but doctors don't always get things right, so I made it my responsibility to educate myself about Inflammatory Breast Cancer and all the treatments I went through. I challenged them, and sometimes went against their advice. But I was in constant sight of my goal - a healthy, happy future with my family."

*

Ann talks about how she used support groups but fundamentally about how she learnt you have to get out there and 'take part'.

"I believe that you know best what is right for you. It is only you that can brush yourself down and get up, even if this is with help. There are groups out there, the support is out there. I have become a member of such a group over the last four years; it's a place to have a rant, ask for suggestions and I've received amazing support. It also gave me a chance to give back to people who are in similar situations. I have made some amazing friends this way and we now support each other. But to find this support you have to be brave and pro-active. You cannot expect people to find you, you need to force yourself out and meet people you don't know, meet people you don't even like, but that just helps to make the friends you do meet even more special."

*

Chrissie's resilience comes through her beliefs and the positive thinking that she applies to each situation that presents itself.

"I believe that every situation is temporary. We all go through challenges but they don't last forever and quite often those challenges have a reason. When I look back now at a lot of the challenges I faced, I brought something positive out of them and quite often that might just be strength of character, it might be the belief that I can get over the next challenge, I'd been strengthened by it. I don't believe that we are ever thrown any challenges that we can't overcome. I believe that those challenges are almost pre-ordained, but they are there to test us and they have a purpose. Have the belief that you *can* do it and that these are just obstacles in a hurdle race."

*

Alison redefined herself after realising that she did not have to remain in the past and be defined by her experiences.

"I came to realise that I didn't have to be that person from the past, I could be whoever I wanted to be. I found hope in a quote from a book by L P Hartley called The Go Between: 'The past is a foreign country, they do things differently there.' In my head I was still that person who was stuck in a violent relationship; I was that person who was not worthy of anything. But I've learnt that actually there are parts of my life that I don't have to keep being; I can be whoever I want to be in the future, I *can* be different and I can do things differently. I don't have to live in the past, with that person I was in the past. I don't have to be that person any more. It's been a long and slow process, but I've now built up a business that I love, I've met a man that I love and who I can completely be myself with and I live without fear that I'm going to disappoint him or that anything is going to go wrong. Finally, I feel like I know who I am, I've got myself back. But I know that I am still very much learning every day and I think there's still a little way to go."

*

Sarah found resilience through stopping, standing still and taking her situation at face value. Tackling it head on brought with it a growth and knowledge of her own capabilities.

"I could describe all of the things that have happened negatively, and perceive what I've done as out of duty or responsibility. I could assume a martyred air of saintly sacrifice. I could resent the hand I had been dealt and I could rail against it. The one thing I couldn't do was refuse to play the hand. Once I had accepted that, I was able to distil all those big and radical changes that seemed out of my reach into microcosms I could apply to my ordinary life.

I could consider, think and plan with so much more clarity. Knee jerk reactions to the slightest problem became considered courses of action. I choose which way I'm travelling now. My trajectory is so much smoother than it was.

Ultimately I celebrate and value my contribution to the lives of those around me. I actually value myself a great deal more than I ever did; I also go a lot easier on myself too. I have faith in my values again and I take pride in not only the achievements of my family but mine too."

Sarah has shaped her experience through changing the way she sees it. I get a real sense of Sarah's journey to make sense of what happened, the impact of it upon her and her struggle to reframe it and to take ownership of it. Through seeing the situation through a lens of positive thinking and gratitude, she has being able to make the situation more meaningful for herself. Dealing with it goes on, the situation goes on, but Sarah's attitude to it can shape how she manages it and understand what she gains from it.

*

Personal Ramblings

Chapter Fifteen - Mantras of the thriving

When we met, Rachel shared her mantra with me and I loved it. "Live love laugh."

> "I just have to remember that I can walk out into the garden and walk on grass and hear the bees and birds and see the Red Arrows flying past! I live in an old RAF house next to where the Red Arrows are based and every time I see them I think yeah – life's alright. Because it's a privilege to be able to see something like that every day – it sounds a bit weird, you know, but they just make me smile. They draw big hearts in the sky across Lincolnshire; it's beautiful and I just think I'd rather not be anywhere else in the world. I also remember that laughter helps so if I'm feeling down I call a friend and I always find that helps. Love is important too – I'm not very good at self-love, that's one thing I'm still struggling with, but I try to remember that there's a lot of love around for me and a lot of people do love me and value me, even if I don't know it or can't see it. I'm sure if I turned around and cried for help there would be hundreds of people who would come and help me because I have helped them in the past and I am very giving of myself to other people. At one stage I asked other people around me what my strengths were and everybody said the one thing they love is that I always remember things and if someone is having a bad day, guaranteed I will send them an email or a

postcard or buy them a present – I send things to people just because it makes me feel good. Our lives are so full these days, so I like to take time to think about friends and let them know that I'm thinking of them too. I don't do this to receive anything back but I know my friends will always be there if I really need them."

Gabby shares her mantras and why they work for her.

'What doesn't kill you makes you stronger'

"Following a cancer diagnosis you are forced to prioritise your life on your own recovery. Many women are not good at putting themselves first, but that is essential for recovery.

'Everything happens for a reason'

I truly believe that sometimes you have to stop fighting against life, go with the flow, and just accept what comes. I trust the universe will provide me with everything I need to make the right decisions. Sometimes you have to be still, stop the internal chatter, and listen to what your heart tells you.

'Thoughts become things, so think good thoughts'

It is amazing how what you focus on comes true for you. If you think about illness, maybe that is what you will attract. I try to focus on wellbeing: physical, emotional and spiritual.

'Live for the moment'

There is no guarantee of tomorrow for any of us, so instead of saving things for best, or struggling until the magical day when we achieve our goal, why not choose to be happy and content today? Don't wait for the perfect moment to do what you want to do - the perfect moment is now."

Chrissie believes:

'Finding your purpose is the key to happiness.'

'Making a choice....you have one. Make it.'

*

Alison has taken some time to reflect upon how she understood what happened to her and how she has grown from it.

"I feel like I've got a whole lifetime to catch up on. I've come to terms with what happened to me in my past and it has affected me. What I've come to realise is that it doesn't have to affect who I am now though. I can take the good bits from it too. I am strong and a survivor.

There were times when I seriously thought that I was going to be killed in that relationship, but I can look back at that now and see that I'm a strong successful person.

If I can survive that and still be happy and smiling and still have faith in life then I can survive anything ... I think!"

"As I said earlier, *"The past is a foreign country, they do things differently there."*

That's my mantra!"

Another favourite mantra that came from both Gabby and Kelly and fits so perfectly with this whole project is:

"My mission in life is not merely to survive,

But to thrive;

And to do so with some humour

And some style."

- Maya Angelou

*

Julie likes:

"If you change the way you look at things, the things you look at change."-

Dr Wayne W Dyer

This is so true and fits in well with positive reframing.

*

Create your own mantras and then make a poster or a journal cover or a postcard. We all have things we've heard and loved that help us make sense of our position, our values, our goal. I have had the same words on a wall in every house for many, many years. I recently bought a stencil of this and it sits on my office wall in beautiful big red letters.

"Dance as though no one is watching

Love as though you've never been hurt

Sing as though no one can hear you

Live as if heaven is on earth."

Take time to reflect on why something means so much to you. It's too easy to read endless quotes but without reflection they're like cheap chocolate. Develop one mantra a day and focus on it for that day. What does it mean for you? How can you change something to adapt to that way of thinking? Who do you know who seems to live like the words suggest? What qualities do they have? Do you have those qualities? Would you like them? Have an internal dialogue with yourself about what you're reading and it will have far more meaning and be far more meaningful in terms of its power in your life.

I love the quote above because it means that I have to try and approach each situation as if it is the first time. My aim is that I choose not to bring all of the baggage and past hurts to each new person, place or thing that I welcome into my life. These words tell me that I have to operate with a deep sense of gratitude for life itself and an appreciation of all that is beautiful.

*

My Mantra For Living Is:

Personal Ramblings

Conclusion – Travelling the path of recovery

When I embarked upon this project, I did so with all my usual naivety and excitement and general lack of planning and a refusal to see any barriers to doing this whatsoever. In learning to embrace all of myself, I have come to accept that there are many reasons in life why this is good (not that they have always been noted as such!) It's far easier to get on with something that is right outside your comfort zone when you live life without a dialogue of sensible sentences floating around your head (I genuinely have very few). Barriers and obstacles just don't exist and my unwavering belief that I can do something if I want to do it means that all those around me trust me and believe me. These are good things.

However, the other side of that coin has been that I often forget to think things through in terms of the impact they have. I hadn't really thought about how painful it would be to delve so deeply into some very old wounds; however healed they may be, they are a part of me and will be with me forever. I now understand that all the writing I have done in the last three years was in preparation for this book so that at the very least I was not exposing my emotional self for the first time, and I had learnt how to articulate my emotional space into the written word with a supportive audience.

One of the hardest moments I had was meeting up with Karen Melton from The Buttle Trust, some 23 years after our first meeting. Bizarrely, I had booked that meeting in the diary as if it were a trip to the dentist and yet I cried solidly for two days after that for the 19 year old girl that I was, desperate for help and some support. We remembered that I had arrived in London with a carrier bag of belongings. We remembered our shopping trip, which was to purchase a gift for me for doing so well. I will be eternally in their debt.

Alongside this road that I have travelled, I have wandered along it with all the women in this book, some of whom were also revisiting places and spaces that they hadn't been to for a while. For some it was too painful and they stepped back so I must thank graciously all the women who put themselves on this journey too. I know every single person in here went through this process for no other reason than they wanted to share their story openly and honestly to try and help anyone else trying to unravel this thing called life, with all its bumpy paths and twists and turns.

In the society that we live, with our endless Facebook updates and messages of pop-happiness, the birth of certain 'professions' with their often simplistic views on the human condition, quotes quotes quotes and more quotes of positivity that are often not reflected upon so just becomes a collection of words resting upon a pretty picture, the message can often be understood that if things are not working for you, you just aren't trying hard enough. You're placing limits on yourself. Your attitude is all wrong. You are the obstacle and you should jolly well brush yourself down and think positively.

I wholeheartedly agree that change comes from within and have supported that view throughout the book. However, the continuing lack of recognition that we live in a complex society as complex human beings and that some people live with adversity every day is patronising, alienating and unhelpful. The offering up of platitudes, endless top tips on how to have instant recovery and a simplistic view of the world needs to be challenged. Adversity isn't a hurdle to be jumped over; for some people they live it every day. The key message is how we work together, building our communities online and offline to support each other to help and enable us to change the way we view our experiences. Then, and only then, can we focus on being part of the solution to reduce the hidden social structures that render some people in a permanent state of dealing with life's traumas.

So do I think we recover? Yes, I do, very much so. Do I think we heal? No, I'm not sure that we do. I think we are complex and we are made up of all the things that happen to us; they create the unique fabric of a person. The journey to recovery can be a trek into long lost places of emotional hurt and while we can believe that we have dealt with it all, there's often the sensation that we are picking open scars that we thought had healed over. While there are still scars, the healing is never complete and the scars are just a part of us, like the lines of wisdom on our faces.

Is there any conclusion to it all? No, I don't think so. The more I know and understand about human beings, our capacity to deal with some of the most horrific incidents and our continuing ability to love and be loved, tells me that there is a continuum and that the journey is the excitement, not an elusive destination.

Most, if not all, of the women I asked to be involved in this project expressed their concern that they just weren't amazing enough. Some of them found it laughable that they might be inspiring. This is itself part of the inspiration. There are enough people out there telling the world that they are special, worth listening to, inspiring, to be aspired to. They don't necessarily inspire me at all.

There is a woman, a friend of mine, who I had asked to be involved in this project but she said that she couldn't, that it was just too painful for her to explore. She lost her first born young son to a car accident four years previously. She later told me that she wasn't inspiring (after I had described her as such); that if I knew the dark places that she went to in her head, I wouldn't say that she was inspiring. Imagine losing your child, your first born, your son, aged 5, to an accident. Imagine where that takes you emotionally every moment of every day. It's almost impossible and unbearable all at once. It's something we won't think about for a single moment because the fear of the pain that we might feel envelopes us so swiftly that it hurts even before the thought has had a moment to work its way through the body.

Every day my friend shows up for life raising her other child. Every day she finds something to smile about. Every day she has to go through the arduous routine of making sense of what has happened in her life. That, to me, is inspiring.

People living their everyday lives, taking life head on, dealing with life on life's terms in a real and honest way with integrity. That inspires me. People who understand abundance to be love, happiness and people, rather than the accumulation of material objects and new kitchens; that inspires me. People quietly yet efficiently seeking to improve the world we live in through turning up every day and seeking to make a difference. That inspires me.

So when you are thinking about what it is to be amazing and inspirational, remember the extraordinariness is in your ordinariness.

*

When I first starting writing regularly, daily, as a means to providing cathartic relief from all the words 'trapped' within me, I had no idea of the response I would get. It was like a key that unlocked not only my emotional space, but that of other people too. I received endless emails from people telling me that they had been able to be open about themselves after reading my story or myblog. This inevitably led me to think about the power of openness and honesty. Only a culture that accepts and understands that to be alive is to have a set of experiences can be a non-judgemental space.

People judge others for all sorts of reasons: ignorance, fear, lack of information, lack of empathy, so developing a culture where sharing our emotions openly, without fear, has to be the way forward. By understanding that we all have experiences, hurts, fears and anxieties, stigmas are reduced, collaborations are formed, friendships cemented, people in need of help are supported and shame will be eliminated. Imagine how we could operate with each other then? Imagine what we could create? Imagine what a space that would be?

Whatever you take from this book, take it with love and may we all join each other on this beautiful walk ...

*

Personal Ramblings

Biographies:

"Alone we can do so little; together we can so much."
Helen Keller

Annett E. Bank

Annett works on the subject of the body in motion as her trademark, expressionist style and designs free-flowing, voluptuous figure paintings, curvy back views, romantic couples and exuberant dancers that stimulate the senses. Her work triggers feelings of aliveness, well-being and revitalisation in the viewer and increases the positive chi energy in people's lives.

After graduating with a BA (Hons) Degree in Fine Art Painting from the University of Brighton, Annett has been studying many metaphysical subjects such as Holistic Counselling, Life Coaching, Colour Therapy, Feng Shui, Reiki, EFT, Exopolitics and psychic stress release. After finishing her art education in 2007 she was selected by the Salon Gallery in Notting Hill, London as one of the UK's Best Graduates and exhibited with Orion Contemporary at various Affordable Art Fairs around the UK and abroad. In 2010 she presented two stunning solo shows at the well-known Brighton Festival and has since had features in publications such as the 'International Holistic Practitioner Association', the 'Soul & Spirit', 'Wise Woman', 'JUNO' and 'The Art of Healing' Magazine about Indigo Energy and the true nature of our reality.

Annett has given talks at the International Indigo & Crystal Children Congress in Germany and writes a highly educational blog, 2012 Ascension Help to support the current spiritual awakening on earth. She also gives creative workshops on finding your soul purpose and Feng Shui as well as hands on ascension guidance. She runs these sessions at the beautiful Monkey Cage Gallery in Ramsgate, Kent, a unique centre for spirituality and contemporary art, which she also co-manages.

www.annett-bank.co.uk

www.monkeycagegallery.co.uk

*

Rani Bilkhu

Rani Bilkhu, mother of five, is the founder and director of Jeena International, an innovative and proactive grassroots women and young people's organisation operating locally, nationally and internationally. For over 20 years Rani has been an activist in community based issues, from interfaith work to gender inequalities for women, especially those who are vulnerable.

She has had many opportunities to utilise her knowledge base and skills by being involved in the Outreach Olympic Committee 2012 for both faith and women. She belongs to the British Adoption and Fostering Organisation (BME group), she's a member of the Independent Advisory Group for Thames Valley Police, a Board Member for The Young Men's Christian Association, Ambassador for Women's Enterprise, and is involved in many consultations for the Government Equalities Office.

Her passion has allowed her to become an entrepreneur with her training company Cultural Insight and, using her knowledge base and skills as a cultural competence consultant and trainer, she has delivered training to the corporate, statutory and third sector. Rani believes that understanding and being able to engage with a diverse range of people will enhance both personal and professional relations; she recognises the grey area between political correctness and relevance of work practice. Rani Bilkhu's views have been aired on Sky News, CNN, Al Jazeera and the BBC.

Rani Bilkhu recognised as third generation India heritage living in the United Kingdom that cultural nuances have not only been impacting both women and young people but also UK policies of how best to safeguard vulnerable people from migrant attitudes, such as forced marriages, honour based violence, gender inequalities, female genital mutilation, domestic abuse, cultural driven violence etc.

Rani Bilkhu will use all her knowledge base and skills to combat injustices and campaign for equality through diverse ways of training, films etc both for women, young people and professionals engaging with BME[11] communities.

Rani Bilkhu, Director and Founder of Jeena International

Email: info@jeenainternational.org

www.jeenainternational.org

---

[11] BME Black Minority Ethnic

Ann Connor

Ann is 43 years old and lives on her own with her three gorgeous children (and loves it). Having two ADHD boys, life is never dull or boring in her house and they all have a lust for life. At the moment Ann is glued to her computer finishing her final year at university and waiting excitedly to see where the next phase of her life will take her.

Ann says: "When I am not studying, we are often to be found getting back to nature, camping around the country, enjoying the scenery of the countryside and our coastline too. I have a passion for natural rather than man-made beauty, so rather than visiting monuments, I would much rather be looking at the beauty of the land and ocean, which links in with my degree on Oceans, Climate and Geology.

When I need some quiet moments for reflection, I am to be found at my local beach, parked up in my VW camper with a cup of tea, at high tide, listening to the sound of the waves and just watching other people's lives go by me."

*

Sarah Crofts

Sarah is 45 years old and lives in London with her nephew, niece, daughter, cat and goldfish. Sarah works full time as an IT specialist.

During spring, summer and autumn Sarah can mostly be found heading away from the city in her campervan with at least one, if not all, of the kids for some free range road tripping with adventures to be had.

Since being involved in Soul Journey, Sarah has been amazed and proud to be involved with so many inspirational women. Sarah's opportunity to contribute also brought about a deep reflection on her life to date and the realisation that, actually, she's doing ok!

Sarah is passionate about her family, her campervan, her friends and her job (not necessarily in that order!) Achieving balance between work and home has been challenging but finding the sweet spot has been so rewarding.

Sarah believes there truly is nothing better than watching a sunset over the ocean from the door of her "café on wheels" (as her daughter calls the campervan!), not least because it signals a new day is on its way with all the opportunities that it holds.

*

Judith Haire

Judith Haire was born in England and graduated from Sheffield University in 1981 with a degree in Political Theory and Institutions. She returned to work in advertising and then spent 11 years in the civil service in Sheffield and London. At 37 her career was cut short when she experienced an acute psychotic episode which was to change her life radically.

Once recovered, she worked in the voluntary sector and

continued to study part time at college. Judith's first article appeared in *Mental Health Practice* magazine in 2007 and her first book *Don't Mind Me* was published in 2008 (Chipmunkapublishing).

Judith has been published in a number of publications including *Mental Health Publishing and Empowerment* (Chipmunkapublishing 2009) and *Our Encounters With Madness* (PCCS Books 2011). She lives by the sea with her husband Ken and cat Smudge and continues to write, blog and study.

Email Judith at judithhaire1@gmail.com

www.judithhaire.com

*

Jayne Hardy

Jayne (who is also known as Jaynie, Janus or Wayner by those closest to her) is 30 years old and lives in Plymouth with her husband, Dominic.

When she's not gorging on chocolate, Jayne works with her husband as a bookkeeper and voluntarily runs a charitable organisation called Blurt (www.blurtitout.org). The idea for Blurt came about from Jayne's personal experiences and provides support for those affected by depression, both directly and indirectly.

A beach loving, sun seeking, sometimes funny but always clumsy lass who enjoys the simple things in life, Jayne is passionate about helping others and raising the awareness of depression. Jayne is at her happiest when she's near the sea.

Being asked to be involved with Soul Journey was an honour which she doesn't always feel worthy of - but that'll be her depression talking ...

"Life is most definitely a rollercoaster – you have to roll with the bad times, the good will come."

www.blurtitout.org

*

Beverley Jones

Following 30 years in corporate senior management Beverley quite literally crashed out in 2009, suffering from ill health. Throughout 2009 / 2010 Beverley travelled on a journey through depression and anxiety which ultimately led to a decision to retrain as a life coach in order to inspire and help others move their lives forward in a positive way. Awaken Life Coaching was founded in 2010 and is an innovative company that wants to help you live your life to its full potential. Beverley says: "It has been so exciting watching my dreams become reality and I'm really looking forward to helping others with theirs."

In June 2012 Beverley launches her book 'Made it Thru the Rain' which chronicles her journey through depression in which she leads you along her personal road to recovery and beyond. In the book Beverley courageously demonstrates how an ordinary life can become extraordinary and how experience can indeed be the greatest gift.

Today, after many years in the city, Beverley can be found enjoying life in her hometown, a small Welsh village where she lives near her parents and is enjoying a relationship with her first boyfriend again.

www.awakenlifecoaching.co.uk

Email: bev@awakenlifecoaching.co.uk

*

Nikki Leader

Nikki is a mother of three with an international corporate background of event organisation, sales and running her own retail business. She has always been intrigued by her own intuitive guidance and the possibilities beyond our imagination and was introduced to the world of energy therapy just before the death of her partner. "I was given the gift of others' clear vision to show me what was possible. When my turn came to review my life I could not have been more grateful for being shown this wisdom."

She founded Awakening Events as a platform for herself and others to share and teach through experiential workshops and lectures that bring spirituality to the forefront for people to look at and introduce into their lives. She also has a practice offering soul plan readings, spiritual guidance and mediumship sittings, meditation groups and animal healing/communication (mainly horses).

Email Nikki at: awakeningevents@btinternet.com
Website: www.nikkileader.co.uk Tel: 07968 552998

*

Christine Lewandowski

Chrissie is slightly over 40 and although she's a born and bred North Easterner, she now lives in Cheshire with her 2 kids, a Cocker and a cat. After years of climbing corporate ladders in various marketing roles, Chrissie finally let go of the financial comfort blanket three years ago to devote her energies into a more satisfying endeavour, Single With Kids, and she now spends most of her weekends and holidays in the company of hundreds of single parent families around the country.

An avid camper and outdoor girl, free time is usually spent in a muddy field somewhere or on the hard shoulder waiting for a kindly AA man to rescue her clapped out but much loved campervan - if happiness is a journey, then it's best savoured in the slow lane. Having spent the last few years trying to convince single parents that life can begin after divorce, Chrissie is delighted that Soul Journey provides the proof that life really can be what you make it, with adversity often proving the greatest lesson and motivation of all.

www.SingleWithKids.co.uk

*

Rachel Linstead

Rachel is 34 years old and lives in the stunning county of Lincolnshire with her beautiful cat Sophie. Rachel wanted to get involved in Soul Journey to share her experiences in life with others to show that anything is possible.

Rachel runs her own business as a nutrition consultant and business coach; she is dedicated to helping business people get the most out of their business. Rachel is a passionate foodie (maybe bordering on an obsession) and enjoys cooking and entertaining using locally sourced produce. When not in the kitchen Rachel enjoys being crafty and will turn her hand to anything that involves sewing, painting, scissors and glitter!!

Rachel enjoys going to the gym and keeping active; she regularly heads to the coast of Lincolnshire for long walks along the beach to take in the fresh sea air and clear her mind.

http://about.me/rachel.linstead

*

Gabby Mottershead

Gabby is the founder of Confidence After Cancer, an organisation that provides coaching and support for women after cancer treatment.

Gabby was inspired to start this support and coaching non-profit organisation after she was diagnosed with a rare and aggressive breast cancer in 2008 at the age of 44. Following chemotherapy, surgeries, and radiotherapy, she suffered with depression and lack of confidence. She realised that there is lots of support for cancer patients during their treatment, but when that ends you are very much alone. She started to connect with other people on Facebook, set up a support group, and was stunned by the number of women who contacted her saying they felt the same and had nowhere to turn.

It is a sobering fact that breast cancer survivors are 37 percent more likely to commit suicide, and depression and anxiety are common (Source the Journal of Cancer Institute) and that this elevated risk continues for at least 25 years after diagnosis.

Gabby provides 121 and group coaching and has been approached by local hospitals to run sessions for them, as the medical teams acknowledge that they are not able to support cancer survivors in the way that they would like to. She is passionate about holistic care, Reiki, NLP, Feng Shui and The Healing Codes, and her mission is to inspire healthy minds and healthy bodies.

Gabby lives in Manchester with her husband Paul, sons Justin and Liam and Annabelle the crazy house rabbit.

Twitter: @gabbymot

Blog: gabbymottershead.wordpress.com

Website: www.confidenceac.co.uk

www.facebook.com/ConfidenceAfterCancer

Alison Neale

Alison is 41 and lives in Oxfordshire with her two teenage kids, her partner, two mad cats and a bearded dragon.

Alison started her career in publishing before taking time out to bring up a family, supplementing the income by doing childminding, bookkeeping and office cleaning. The turn of the millennium was the turning point for her: within ten years she left a violent relationship and became a single parent; did a degree; got married and divorced; and started her own business.

Nowadays Alison masquerades as The Proof Fairy, providing editing, blogging, social media and web services to authors, charities and small businesses. She's a regular business networker; she's also a moderator for her local Freecycle group, a regular blood donor and supporter of various charitable organisations including Plan and the British Heart Foundation.

Alison loves football, motorsports and music and she's also a keen amateur photographer and can often be found tramping round the Oxfordshire countryside on photo treks with her partner.

Alison wanted to be involved in Soul Journey as she feels that every woman has the strength to thrive when dealt a bad hand of cards, and she wanted her story to inspire others. Since taking part in the project she has felt an increase in her own confidence and she's now starting to develop her business to include public speaking, something she once felt she could never do!

At one stage Alison wondered what the point of life was; now she embraces every day and is on a mission to experience as much as she can – recently she's driven a single seater racing car, scuba dived and walked on fire!

Alison's business: www.theprooffairy.com

Alison's personal blog: www.alisonneale.co.uk

*

Sue Ritchie

Sue decided early in life to tear up the map that others had written for her, and make her own. Her map has taken her out of the council estate, across the world to live and work in the jungles of Asia and Central America with her young son, and then back to the UK, where she now lives. She has shown time and time again that with determination, vision and faith in oneself, anything is possible. She's a down-to-earth, ordinary woman who has proved that an extraordinary life can spring from humble beginnings.

After 18 years in the education sector, Sue is now a qualified personal and business coach who runs You Time Coaching where she helps professional women to develop the confidence to be brilliant in the workplace. She provides 1:1 confidence mentoring and bespoke workshops as well as delivering her signature talk, 'Stories from the suitcase: strategies for being brilliant'. Sue also writes a successful blog and regularly guest blogs for others, including Virgin Media.

She currently lives in Lincoln with her son who is now 18, and her husband whom she met whilst overseas. She has hung up her boots, unpacked the suitcase, and now loves nothing better than to spend time at home with her family before her son goes off to university later this year.

Sue can be found at www.youtimecoaching.co.uk, where you'll be able to find out just how she can inspire you to be brilliant.

*

Kelly Short

Kelly Short is a chatty and outgoing young woman who loves life. She lives in Kent with her husband Toby and together they spend much of their time renovating their home. Although more accurately Kelly makes the decisions whilst Toby does the hard work under her ever watchful eye!

In 2006 Kelly and Toby were planning a future together. However, their lives changed forever when they received the devastating news that Kelly, aged 31, had breast cancer. Physically she coped well with the treatment that followed, but the psychological impact was much harder to bear. Having lost her hair, her breast and her zest for life, Kelly struggled to cope with her new body image.

In the spring of 2008 Kelly appeared on the C4 programme How To Look Good Naked. The decision to take part in the show was to change her life forever. Having accepted her post cancer body, Kelly started modelling post surgery lingerie. Before taking part in the show Kelly's confidence was so low she could hardly bear to leave the house. Now you can see pictures of her on the web in her undies!

Despite a setback with her health following a recent reocurrence, the body confidence has remained and Kelly is back to her talkative, confident self.

As well as modelling, Kelly has trained bra fitters in how to deal with customers who have had breast surgery. She gets a great deal of satisfaction from helping fitters to understand the needs of the customer who has had breast cancer. She has also spoken at a number of events on the subject of body confidence after breast cancer. Kelly speaks regularly for Breast Cancer Care and is a dedicated supporter of the charity that provides information and support for anyone affected by breast cancer.

Kelly now embraces life fully whilst trying to balance a healthy lifestyle with eating cake!

Follow Kelly on Twitter: @kelly_talks

Or take a look at what Kelly is up to on her website: www.kellytalks.com

See pictures of Kelly modelling at

www.royce-lingerie.co.uk

Find help and support for anyone affected by breast cancer at www.breastcancercare.org.uk

*

Julie Southgate

Do you live in the present moment? Do you struggle with forgiveness or a lack of self-worth? Are you led by your heart or your head? These are all questions that can be reflected on and brought into conscious awareness. Julie has gained conscious awareness since coming to terms with a painful marriage break up and the journey that followed.

Julie lives in Lowestoft, Suffolk with her husband and two children. On leaving school Julie trained and worked as a nursery nurse in a local school from 1989–2010. Her desire to work in such a caring profession extended from helping children to wanting to be of help to adults too, so Balanced Health Ltd was created in the summer of 2010 offering a range of holistic therapies.

In her spare time Julie enjoys dog walking, meditation, going to the gym, yoga, cinema, theatre and spending time with family and friends. Since being involved in Soul Journey Julie has been working on a new website for her company and realising that the world really is her oyster!

Email:Julie@balancedhealthltd.co.uk

www.Balancedhealthltd.co.uk

*

Amy Trevaskus

Amy is 32 years old and lives in Somerset with her husband. Amy has always written, be it short stories, poetry, children's stories or novels for adults. She runs her own creative copywriting agency, runs The Blue Room and cares for her dad who has Progressive Supranuclear Palsy.

Being involved in Soul Journey has made Amy extremely proud of what she and her whole family have achieved in such a small amount of time!

Amy is passionate about writing, reading, family and friends and gets her laughs mainly from her husband who has been a total star even though life has been tough over the past few years. Life is complicated but full of love.

Amy has been an active fundraiser for the charity that supports people who are affected by Progressive Supranuclear Palsy – Amy and her husband completed a week long 'Arctic Adventure' to help raise money for The PSP Association. If you would like to find out more about Progressive Supranuclear Palsy you can visit www.pspeur.org.

If you would like to find out about The Blue Room you can visit www.theblue-room.co.uk and to find out about Amy's children's books you can visit;

www.pingandpongbooks.co.uk

*

Suggested Reading

How To Heal Your Life by Louise Hay

The Road Less Travelled by M. Scott Peck

The Celestine Prophecy by James Redfield

Families and How to Survive Them by John Cleese and Robyn Skinner

The Power by Rhonda Bryn

The Artist's Way by Julia Cameron

Feel the Fear & Do It Anyway by Susan Jeffers

The Power of Now by Eckhart Tolle

How Full is Your Bucket? by Tom Rath and Donald O. Clifton PhD

Think and Grow Rich by Napoleon Hill

Healing The Shame That Binds You by John Bradshaw

The Art of Happiness by The Dalai Lama

Goddess by Elizabeth Wilson

Soul Journey
The Greatest Secrets To Living The Life You Want

Lisa Cherry: About the author

Who is Lisa Cherry? To those who meet her, it's impossible to define her in a single sentence. At first glance, she's a successful businesswoman running a holistic massage practice. However, if you spoke to her clients you would discover that she doesn't merely relieve stress or pain, but empowers women to make positive lifelong changes.

Lisa set up Holistic Health in February 2010 convinced that by offering a spectrum of health treatments people would be enabled to lead a healthier, more balanced and happier life. Shortly after, this vision for helping people motivated her and a friend to establish a networking organisation, Networking Women. Initially aimed at supporting local women to have the confidence to grow their business, Lisa's infectious personality transformed monthly meetings into a hub of positivity where women drew inspiration from themselves and each other.

Within one year, as membership expanded across Oxfordshire, Gloucestershire and Wiltshire, Networking Women become a thriving influential enterprise. Lisa herself was nominated in 2011 for a Divine Women award for selflessly making a real difference to women's lives. She achieved all this whilst raising two children as a single parent.

Lisa herself has overcome adversity despite facing many challenging life experiences. Her teenage years were symbolised by hurtling from one foster home to the next seeking stability and love. School exclusions, care homes, alcoholism and homelessness left their mark, before Lisa found the inner strength to break free from a spiral of self-destruction and chose life instead.

After getting sober at the age of 20, steely determination drove her through a university degree, after which she devoted 18 years to the social services sector helping children and families through difficult times – whilst still battling her own inner demons.

It was through pursuing a holistic approach to life that Lisa found the roots of her true recovery. With a holistic massage diploma in the bag, her thirst for life was unleashed. Far from being a mere survivor, Lisa's passion for life, change and personal development now inspires others to follow their dreams.

In fact, upon discovering blogging, she rapidly connected with an audience hungry to listen and, like Lisa, confront tough challenges in their own past. With her encouragement many women embarked on their own journey of discovery, sharing their achievements with Lisa on her blog.

What makes Lisa so compelling is her selfless ability to openly share her soul, reflecting upon life with complete honesty and integrity. Imbuing others with a vision for change, she empowers others in their own healing; such is the effect that Lisa's boundless energy and incredible positivity have on all those whose lives she touches. In this, her first book, Lisa reveals her own mantra for living and shares other women's celebratory journeys over adversity.